# TWENTIETH CENTURY VIEWS

The aim of this series is to present the best in contemporary critical opinion on major authors, providing a twentieth century perspective on their changing status in an era of profound revaluation.

Maynard Mack, *Series Editor*
Yale University

# A. E. HOUSMAN

## A COLLECTION OF CRITICAL ESSAYS

Edited by

*Christopher Ricks*

Prentice-Hall, Inc.  *Englewood Cliffs, N. J.*
A SPECTRUM BOOK

Current printing (last number):
10   9   8   7   6   5   4   3   2   1

# Acknowledgments

Quotations from A. E. Housman are reprinted by permission of:

The Society of Authors as the literary representative of the Estate of the late A. E. Housman, and Jonathan Cape Ltd., English publishers of A. E. Housman's *Collected Poems*.

Charles Scribner's Sons, for *My Brother, A. E. Housman* by Laurence Housman. Copyright 1937, 1938 Laurence Housman; renewal copyright © 1965, 1966 Lloyds Bank Limited.

Holt, Rinehart & Winston, Inc., for *The Collected Poems of A. E. Housman*. Copyright 1922 by Holt, Rinehart & Winston, Inc. Copyright 1936, 1950 by Barclays Bank Ltd. Copyright © 1964 by Robert E. Symons. And for "A Shropshire Lad"—Authorized Edition—from *The Collected Poems of A. E. Housman*. Copyright 1939, 1940, © 1959 by Holt, Rinehart & Winston, Inc. Copyright © 1967 by Robert E. Symons. Cambridge University Press, for A. E. Housman, *Selected Prose*. Copyright © 1961 by Cambridge University Press.

# Contents

The Housman Dilemma, *by John Sparrow*                      163

# A. E. HOUSMAN

# Introduction

*by Christopher Ricks*

## I

The poems of A. E. Housman disrupt all the usual allegiances. Edith Sitwell can join with F. R. Leavis, George Meredith, and Hugh Kenner in disapproval of the author of *A Shropshire Lad,* while William Empson can concur with H. W. Garrod, John Sparrow, and G. K. Chesterton—who, with numerical oddity, called Housman "one of the one or two great classic poets of our time." W. B. Yeats expressed a grudging admiration: "*A Shropshire Lad* is worthy of its fame, but a mile further and all had been marsh." It was left to T. S. Eliot to perform his accustomed feat of balancing. His review of *The Name and Nature of Poetry* (a review which Dr. Leavis called an "ambiguous piece of correctness") is respectful, distant, and the equivocal work of Old Possum:

> Observation leads me to believe that different poets may compose in very different ways; my experience (for what that is worth) leads me to believe that Mr. Housman is recounting the authentic processes of a real poet. "I have seldom," he says, "written poetry unless I was rather out of health." I believe that I understand that sentence. If I do, it is a guarantee—if any guarantee of that nature is wanted— of the quality of Mr. Housman's poetry.

The quality of Housman's poetry, acknowledged by Mr. Eliot, is no longer assured of recognition. The force that was once felt in *A Shropshire Lad* was not always purely acknowledged in straight literary criticism—it was acknowledged in some bizarre and non-literary ways, as the following anecdote about Housman makes clear:[1]

> He also told me that Clarence Darrow, the U.S.A. lawyer, insisted on coming to Cambridge to him as he had got off so many possible murderers by quoting poems out of *A Shropshire Lad* in support of his arguments: he showed Housman reports which bore this out. In particular "The Culprit" (which, incidentally, is in *Last Poems*) had been useful. The poem reads:
>
> > But fetch the county kerchief;
> > And noose me in the knot,
> > And I will rot.
>
> But the "county kerchief" in Mr. Darrow's mouth had become the "County Sheriff"—"Fetch the County Sheriff, &c"!

Housman himself said that Loeb and Leopold owed their life sentence partly to him. It is a curious tribute to his poems, though it is one about which he is likely to have been of two minds. He was not the sort of man who is unequivocally opposed to capital punishment, and he believed that "Revenge is a valuable passion, and the only sure pillar on which justice rests."

But the approbation accorded to Housman's poetry is not just a matter of the courtroom, nor—at the opposite extreme—is it simply that "academic approbation, which is the second death" (the words are Housman's). This collection of essays hopes to make clear what it was that could lead Mr. Empson to begin his review of *More Poems* with the words: "It is long since I cut pages with more curiosity and expectation than I did these, and they are not disappointing."

Mr. Empson's excited admiration is ultimately easier to comprehend than Mr. Kenner's excited contempt. Mr. Kenner[2] can complain that Housman is "melodramatic" and then find in some innocent lines an appeal to "necrophily, mother-hunger, and adolescent heroics." He can ridicule Housman's phrasing while replacing with words of his own choice the two most important words in Housman's thirteen.

---

[1] Grant Richards, *Housman 1897–1936* (London: Oxford University Press, 1941), p. 244.

[2] Hugh Kenner, *The Poetry of Ezra Pound* (New York: New Directions; London: Faber & Faber, 1951), pp. 67, 228.

## II

> To judge of poets is only the faculty of poets; and not of all poets, but the best.

So the poets have told us, from Ben Jonson to T. S. Eliot. Without being too credulous about poet-critics, we might nevertheless believe that Housman's claim on our attention is manifest in the attention he has elicited from other poets. Housman is a poet about whom poets write poems—W. H. Auden, Ezra Pound, Kingsley Amis (and Witter Bynner, E. H. W. Meyerstein, and Paul Engle). Some of the most appreciative criticism on Housman is by Randall Jarrell, Richard Wilbur, Robert Graves, and William Empson. Other poets—John Crowe Ransom, John Peale Bishop, Stephen Spender, John Wain—may have had severe reservations about the value of Housman's poems, but for each of them Housman was a poet worth applying one's mind to.

The point would not much matter if there weren't the widespread idea that Housman's poems are nothing more than the literature of those who don't really care about literature. Maiden aunts and old-world dons are thought to be "fond of" Housman, as they are fond of detective stories. So there hangs about Housman's reputation a fatal combination of the musty and the bright-eyed, as of elaborate bindings at school prize-givings. What better gift (at once cultural and innocuous) than *The Rubáiyát of Omar Khayyám* or *A Shropshire Lad* or the poems of Kahlil Gibran? But Edward FitzGerald is more of a poet than that, and Housman is more of a poet than FitzGerald.

It is true that Housman's work sometimes pays a price for the wide appeal that it seeks—Housman sometimes makes a poem too instantly palatable. (Not that this is a worse fault than the determined unpalatability of some present-day verse.) Like Edna St. Vincent Millay, and John Betjeman, Housman is the kind of poet easily overrated by the middlebrow many, and easily underrated by the highbrow few. A century ago the most popular of Victorian poets threw out an impromptu reflection on popularity. Tennyson knew that the other barrel of the gun gets you if the first misses:

Popular, Popular, Unpopular!
"You're no Poet"—the critics cried!
"Why?" said the Poet. "You're unpopular!"
Then they cried at the turn of the tide—
"You're no Poet!" "Why?"—"You're popular!"
Pop-gun, Popular and Unpopular!

One hope of the present collection is to disentangle Housman from the jealous embrace of a certain kind of admirer. Just as Jane Austen is too good a writer to be left to "The Janeites," so in the 1960's Housman needs to be protected against some of his friends. In 1929 H. W. Garrod could begin a lecture on Housman: "I have confessed before to a fondness for the poetry of Fellows of colleges." Even those with a soft spot for donnishness and nostalgia may feel that, with friends like Garrod, Housman's poems don't need enemies.

But popularity—and in particular popularity with those who are unpopular—is only one of the things that needlessly come between Housman and a certain kind of modern reader. "Adolescent": that is the word used with quite different valuations by critics as different as R. P. Blackmur, George Orwell, Conrad Aiken, W. H. Auden, and Hugh Kenner. What exactly do we mean by "adolescent," and is it simply a pejorative word? These are precisely the issues which some of the critics here have felt obliged to consider. Mr. Auden (in the *New Statesman,* May 18, 1957) spoke clearly and firmly:

It has often been said that Housman is a poet of adolescence, and this is fair enough as long as this judgment is not meant to imply, as it usually is, that nobody over the age of twenty-one can or should enjoy reading him. To grow up does not mean to outgrow either childhood or adolescence but to make use of them in an adult way. But for the child in us, we should be incapable of intellectual curiosity; but for the adolescent, of serious feeling for other individuals. I can imagine a person who had "outgrown" both, though I have never met one; he would be a completely social official being with no personal identity. All that a mature man can give his child and adolescent in return for what they keep giving him are humility, humour, charity and hope. He will never teach them to despise any strong passion, however strange and limited, or to reject a poet, like Housman, who gives it utterance.

Yet Housman's reputation has suffered from a misconception. Consider T. S. Eliot on Shelley, in *The Use of Poetry and the Use of Criticism*:

> The ideas of Shelley seem to me always to be ideas of adolescence— as there is every reason why they should be. And an enthusiasm for Shelley seems to me also to be an affair of adolescence: for most of us, Shelley has marked an intense period before maturity, but for how many does Shelley remain the companion of age?

The mistaken assumption has been that "adolescent" poems are what adolescents enjoy. The opposite is the case. They are what yesterday's adolescents enjoyed. Mr. Eliot tells us that he was "intoxicated by Shelley's poetry at the age of fifteen, and now finds it almost unreadable"—and what effect was that remark sure to have on fifteen-year-olds? No self-respecting adolescent is likely to give his time to literature that his elders describe as written for, or appealing to, the likes of him. None of us likes to be thought of as "the likes of." It is true that poets like Housman and Shelley have in the past had a potent appeal to the young—but that was mainly because their claims and concerns seemed vividly adult. But once the appeal to the young is bruited abroad, the whirligig of time brings in its revenges, and the young are quick to move on. That Housman is a poet of adolescence, Mr. Auden truly remarks, shouldn't mean "that nobody over the age of twenty-one can or should enjoy reading him." But the actual situation is harshly the opposite: it is only those *over* twenty-one who read Housman or Shelley (by choice), since for the young the poems of Housman and Shelley have been too brutally stamped "for the young." The problem for those who wish to get Housman's poems a fair hearing is now the opposite of what it used to be. When George Orwell said, "Such poems might have been written expressly for adolescents," he pointed directly—though silently—at the reason why the average age of Housman's admirers is in danger of getting higher every year. It is not much consolation that the same is probably true of the average age of admirers of *The Cantos*.

John Sparrow could say in 1937:

> Because it expresses authentically the emotions, above all the unhappiness, of youth, and because its form is easy and its content has

the charm of the simple, at times of the sentimental, his verse appeals
almost unfailingly to those who themselves are young.

Not any more, it doesn't—not once the word has gone out that
this is the ticket upon which Housman's poems are offered. The
mistake is surely to assume that the qualities that appeal to youth
and adolescence are constant, rather than a whirligig. Do the young
still delight in literature of which the "form is easy," with "the
charm of the simple, at times of the sentimental"? The hungry
generations tread this down.

The audience that needs to be captured for Housman is precisely
the one of which he is supposed to be already in possession: he *does*
already enjoy the esteem of those so-called "New Critics" who are
supposed to be the enemies of his kind of poetry: Cleanth Brooks,
William Empson, Randall Jarrell.


# III


It is the poems which matter most—and all the more so in a
collection of essays such as this. Yet Housman was not only a
haunting poet (the adjective is Mr. Empson's), but also a haunting
figure. Proud and cruelly witty, he was a man whose reticence,
arrogance, and will-power are fascinating and unforgettable. It
would be wrong to use his poems *solely* as biographical documents,
but there is no reason why they should not be used *also* as biographical documents.

The best insight into this enigmatic and daunting figure was
provided by Edmund Wilson (see p. 22):

> Housman's anger is tragic like Swift's. He is perhaps more pitiable
> than Swift, because he has been compelled to suppress himself more
> completely.

Housman quoted with grim pleasure Swift's remark that "The
bulk of mankind is as well qualified for flying as for thinking,"
and Housman too was lacerated by *saeva indignatio*. So that it
makes a strange and illuminating exercise to bring together from
Dr. Johnson's life of Swift a cento of quotations all insistently

relevant to Housman. For the opening quotations from Johnson, it is sufficient to remember that Housman at first failed his B. A. Honours entirely; that he then gained a mere Pass degree; and that in his fierce leisure he made himself "the Latin Scholar of his generation."

> In his academical studies he was either not diligent or not happy. It must disappoint every reader's expectation, that, when at the usual time he claimed the Bachelorship of Arts, he was found by the examiners too conspicuously deficient for regular admission, and obtained his degree at last by *special favour;* a term used in that university to denote want of merit. Of this disgrace it may be easily supposed that he was much ashamed, and shame had its proper effect in producing reformation. He resolved from that time to study eight hours a day, and continued his industry for seven years, with what improvement is sufficiently known.
>
> For some time after, Swift was probably employed in solitary study, gaining the qualifications requisite for future eminence.
>
> The thoughts of death rushed upon him, at this time, with such incessant importunity, that they took possession of his mind, when he first waked, for many years together.
>
> His asperity continually increasing, condemned him to solitude; and his resentment of solitude sharpened his asperity. He was not, however, totally deserted: some men of learning . . . often visited him; and he wrote from time to time either verse or prose. . . . He is supposed to have felt no discontent when he saw them printed.
>
> A mind incessantly attentive, and, when it was not employed upon great things, busy with minute occurrences.
>
> In his seventy-eighth year, he expired.
>
> His delight was in simplicity. That he has in his works no metaphor, as has been said, is not true; but his few metaphors seem to be received rather by necessity than choice. He studied purity.
>
> Instead of wishing to seem better, he delighted in seeming worse than he was.
>
> He had a countenance sour and severe, which he seldom softened by any appearance of gaiety.
>
> A man of a rigorous temper, with that vigilance of minute attention which his works discover.

Whatever he did, he seemed willing to do in a manner peculiar to himself, without sufficiently considering that singularity, as it implies a contempt of the general practice, is a kind of defiance which justly provokes the hostility of ridicule.

He indulged his disposition to petulance and sarcasm, and thought himself injured if the licentiousness of his raillery, the freedom of his censures, or the petulance of his frolics, was resented or repressed. He predominated over his companions with very high ascendency, and probably would bear none over whom he could not predominate.

He habitually affects a style of arrogance, and dictates rather than persuades. This authoritative and magisterial language he expected to be received as his peculiar mode of jocularity; but he apparently flattered his own arrogance by an assumed imperiousness.

He delighted in doing what he knew himself to do well.

He was not a man to be either loved or envied. He seems to have wasted life in discontent, by the rage of neglected pride, and the languishment of unsatisfied desire. He is querulous and fastidious, arrogant and malignant; he scarcely speaks of himself but with indignant lamentations, or of others but with insolent superiority when he is gay, and with angry contempt when he is gloomy.

[The poems] are, for the most part, what their author intended. The diction is correct, the numbers are smooth, and the rhymes exact. There seldom occurs a hard-laboured expression, or a redundant epithet; all his verses exemplify his own definition of a good style, they consist of *proper words in proper places*.

Perhaps no writer can easily be found that . . . in all his excellences and all his defects has so well maintained his claim to be considered as original.

Even when we allow that Housman is a far smaller writer than Swift, can it be said of Housman that he was "original"? The wittiest answer was given by Housman himself, when in 1928 he sent a message to A. J. A. Symons, refusing to give permission for his poems to appear in an anthology of the Nineties:

He may be consoled, and also amused, if you tell him that to include me in an anthology of the Nineties would be just as technically correct, and just as essentially inappropriate, as to include Lot in a book on Sodomites.[3]

[3] *Housman 1897–1936*, p. 245.

## IV

A sketch of the contributions to this volume. First, there are three poems about Housman, by W. H. Auden, Ezra Pound, and Kingsley Amis. Next come three essays which particularly stress the relationship between Housman the man and Housman the poet: Edmund Wilson's evocation of the essential Housman; John Wain's consideration of the pressures that the academic life puts upon a poet; and W. H. Auden's succinct speculations on Housman as the intellectual divided against himself.

The central group of essays focuses more upon the poems than upon the poet. "Housman: A Controversy" consists of Cyril Connolly's article on Housman in 1936, followed by the retorts which it excited. In "Texts from Housman" Randall Jarrell offers a lovingly detailed analysis of two of Housman's best poems. Cleanth Brooks's anniversary tribute ranges widely through all the poems, and is especially concerned with bringing to bear the right comparisons. In "Round About A Poem of Housman's" Richard Wilbur radiates from the poem (without quitting it) into a discussion of poetry today, contrasting Yeats and Pound with the tact of Housman's "art of referring." Next, the essay by this editor tries to show the relationship between Housman's best poems and his famous (notorious?) lecture on *The Name and Nature of Poetry*. Morton Dauwen Zabel surveys "The Whole of Housman" in a compacted account of the poet's "subtle and ennobling lyric dignity." In "The Poetry of Emphasis," F. W. Bateson studies Housman's style in detail, remarking Housman's attempt to match the verbal density of Latin.

It is the professor of Latin who is the focus of J. P. Sullivan's protest against "the intensely English cult of A. E. Housman as a scholar, poet, and personality." Combative but at least not condescending, this protest sharpens one's sense of the important issues —cultural, educational, and social—involved in Housman's influence upon classical studies. Finally, there is John Sparrow's "The Housman Dilemma." Valuable for its account of the problems raised by Housman's manuscripts, it stands too as a living instance of the kind of work to which Housman himself dedicated so much of his life. "The faintest of all human passions is the love of truth," said Housman, and there would be something missing from any collection that did not try to show that this passion need not be faint. All the better, then, if the subject matter can be the most appropriate of instances: the text of Housman's own poems.

# A. E. Housman

## by W. H. Auden

No one, not even Cambridge, was to blame
(Blame if you like the human situation):
Heart-injured in North London, he became
The Latin Scholar of his generation.

Deliberately he chose the dry-as-dust,
Kept tears like dirty postcards in a drawer;
Food was his public love, his private lust
Something to do with violence and the poor.

In savage foot-notes on unjust editions
He timidly attacked the life he led,
And put the money of his feelings on

The uncritical relations of the dead,
Where only geographical divisions
Parted the coarse hanged soldier from the don.

"A. E. Housman." From W. H. Auden, *Collected Shorter Poems 1927–1957* (New York: Random House, Inc.; London: Faber & Faber). © Copyright 1966 by W. H. Auden. Reprinted by permission of W. H. Auden, Random House, Inc., and Faber & Faber. This poem was first published in *New Writing*, Spring, 1939, and then in *Another Time* (1940).

# Mr. Housman's Message

## by Ezra Pound

O woe, woe,
People are born and die,
We also shall be dead pretty soon
Therefore let us act as if we were
                dead already.

The bird sits on the hawthorn tree
But he dies also, presently.
Some lads get hung, and some get shot.
Woeful is this human lot.
            *Woe! woe, etcetera.* . . .

London is a woeful place,
Shropshire is much pleasanter.
Then let us smile a little space
Upon fond nature's morbid grace.
        *Oh, Woe, woe, woe, etcetera.* . . .

# A.E.H.

## by Kingsley Amis

Flame the westward skies adorning
Leaves no like on field or hill;
Sounds of battle joined at morning
Wane and wander and are still.

Past the standards rent and muddied,
Past the random heaps of slain,
Stalks a redcoat who, unbloodied,
Weeps with fury, not from pain.

Wounded lads, when to renew them
Death and surgeons cross the shade,
Still their cries, hug darkness to them;
All at last in sleep are laid.

All save one who nightlong curses
Wounds imagined more than seen,
Who in level tones rehearses
What the fact of wounds must mean.

"A.E.H." From Kingsley Amis, *A Look Round the Estate* (London: Jonathan Cape Limited, 1967). © Copyright 1967 by Kingsley Amis. This poem was first published in *Listen*, IV, Autumn, 1962. Reprinted by permission of Kingsley Amis and George Hartley.

# A. E. Housman

## by *Edmund Wilson*

*The voice, sent forth, can never be recalled.*

When A. E. Housman's *Introductory Lecture* delivered in 1892 "Before the Faculties of Arts and Laws and of Science in University College, London" was reprinted in 1933, Housman characteristically wrote of it as follows: "The Council of University College, not I, had the lecture printed." He described it as "rhetorical and not wholly sincere" and put upon the title page, *Nescit vox missa reverti.*

The little essay is curious in largely evading the questions it raises and taking the direction of a piece of special pleading for the author's own pursuits. Both the sciences and the arts, says Housman, are ordinarily defended by arguments which make their interests appear mutually antagonistic. But the arguments on both sides are mistaken. Science is said to be useful; but what is the use, for example, of a great deal of astronomical research? And the businessmen who make practical use of the results of scientific study are usually not scientists at all. (They do make use of them, nevertheless; and the results of the most gratuitous researches are always likely to turn out to be useful.) The Humanities, on the other hand, are supposed to "transform and beautify our inner nature by culture." Yet the proportion of the human race capable of being benefited by classical studies is certainly very small, and these "can attain the desired end without that minute and accurate study of the classical tongues which affords Latin professors their only ex-

cuse for existing." Not even the great critics of the classics are
genuine classical scholars: "When it comes to literary criticism,
heap up in one scale all the literary criticism that the whole nation
of professed scholars ever wrote, and drop into the other the thin
green volume of Matthew Arnold's *Lectures on Translating Homer,*
which has long been out of print because the British public does
not care to read it, and the first scale, as Milton says, will straight
fly up and kick the beam." (We shall look into the assumptions
here in a moment.)

The arts and the sciences alike are only to be defended, says
Housman, on the ground that the desire for knowledge is one of
the normal human appetites, and that men suffer if they do not
have it gratified. And "once we have recognized that knowledge in
itself is good for man, we shall need to invent no pretexts for
studying this subject or that; we shall import no extraneous considerations of use or ornament to justify us in learning one thing
rather than another. If a certain department of knowledge specially
attracts a man, let him study that, and study it because it attracts
him; and let him not fabricate excuses for that which requires no
excuse, but rest assured that the reason why it most attracts him is
that it is best for him."

This is certainly true in so far as it means that we should follow
the direction of our aptitudes; but it seems to imply that there is
no difference in value between one department of learning and another or between the different points of view from which the various kinds of research can be conducted. There is no conception in
Housman's mind, as there would have been in Whitehead's, for
example, of relating the part to the whole, understanding the or-
ganism through the cell. Knowledge seems to be regarded by Housman as a superior sort of pastime—"good for man" because it gives
him pleasure and at most because "it must in the long run be
better for a man to see things as they are than to be ignorant of
them; just as there is less fear of stumbling or of striking against
corners in the daylight than in the dark." (*"The thoughts of others
Were light and fleeting, Of lovers' meeting Or luck or fame. Mine
were of trouble, And mine were steady, So I was ready When
trouble came."*) The disillusionment of western man in regard to

his place in the universe, finding "that he has been deceived alike
as to his origin and his expectations, that he neither springs of the
high lineage he fancied, nor will inherit the vast estate he looked
for," is described in an eloquent passage; and the activities of the
"Arts and Laws and Science" are finally characterized as "the
rivalry of fellow soldiers in striving which can most victoriously
achieve the common end of all, to set back the frontier of darkness."

In other words, there is no role for creation in Housman's scheme
of things. Indeed, if one had read only his poetry, one might be
surprised to find that he even believed that it was possible or of any
importance to set back the frontier of darkness. In this poetry, we
find only the realization of man's smallness on his turning globe
among the other revolving planets and of his own basic wrongness
to himself, his own inescapable anguish. No one, it seems, can do
anything about this universe which "ails from its prime foundation": we can only, like Mithridates, render ourselves immune to
its poisons by compelling ourselves to absorb them in small quan-
tities in order that we may not succumb to the larger doses reserved
for us by our fellows, or face the world with the hard mask of
stoicism, "manful like the man of stone." For the rest, "let us
endure an hour and see injustice done." And now we learn that
for Housman knowledge itself meant at most the discovery of
things that were already there—of those sharp corners which it
was just as well not to bump into, of facts that were as invariable
and as inert as the astronomical phenomena which are always
turning up in his poems and form the subject of the poem of
Manilius to which he devoted so much of his life. He does not look
to the sciences and arts for the births of new worlds of thought, of
new possibilities for men themselves. It is characteristic of him that
he should speak, in this essay, of Milton as a greater artist than
Shakespeare, of Shakespeare, in fact, as not "a great artist"—as if
the completeness and richness of Shakespeare's dramatic imagination, a kind of genius which Milton, by comparison, seems hardly
to possess at all, were not important enough to be taken into account in estimating his greatness as an artist—as if those stretches
of *Paradise Lost* where everything is dead but the language were
not the result of artistic deficiency. Again, the creation of life has
no place in the universe of Housman.

Housman's practice in his own field of scholarship is an astonishing proof of this. The modern English classical scholar of the type of A. W. Verrall or Gilbert Murray is a critic not merely of texts but of the classics in their quality as literature and of literature in its bearing on history. This school on one of its sides sometimes merges with the anthropology of J. G. Frazer; and it deals with ancient Greece and Rome in relation to the life of its own time, restates them in terms of its own time. The danger, of course, with a Verrall or a Murray is that, with something of the poet's imagination himself, he may give way, in the case of Greek drama, for example, to inventing new plays of his own and trying to foist them on Euripides or Aeschylus. With Housman we do not run this danger. Housman is the opposite kind of scholar; he is preoccupied with the emendation of texts. He could never have been guilty of the extravagances of a Gilbert Murray or a Verrall, but he was not capable of their kind of illumination. Note his assumption, in the passage quoted above, that "the minute and accurate study of the classical tongues," with which he himself is exclusively preoccupied, "affords Latin professors their only excuse for existing." Have those classical scholars who write history, who write criticism, who make translations—Gibbon and Renan and Verrall and Murray and Jowett and Mackail (to take in the whole field of the classics)—no excuse for existing, then? Is it so certain that, if their literary criticism were put into the scales with Matthew Arnold on Homer, the scholars would kick the beam? Or are such persons not scholars at all? In either case, it is plain that, for Housman, their activities lie outside the periphery of the sphere which he has chosen for himself.

Not, however, that Housman in this limited sphere has left the poet of *A Shropshire Lad* behind him. On the contrary, the peculiar genius which won him a place beside Porson and Bentley, which established him in his own time as almost supreme, with, apparently, only Wilamowitz as a rival, was derived from his ability to combine with the most "minute and accurate" mastery of language a first-hand knowledge of how poets express themselves. "The task of editing the classics," he wrote in his preface to Juvenal, "is continually attempted by scholars who have neither enough intellect nor enough literature. Unless a false reading chances to be unmetrical or ungrammatical they have no means of knowing that it is false." And he himself seemed able with a miraculous sureness to give the authors back their lines as they had written them. So, for example, despite a unanimity of manuscripts which read *"Omnis ab hac cura mens relavata mea est,"* Housman restored to Ovid from an inscription one of the latter's characteristic turns of style: *"Omnis ab hac cura cura levata mea est."* (*"And set you at your threshold down, Townsman of a stiller town"*; *"Runners whom renown outran And the name died before the man"*; *"By Sestos town, in Hero's tower, On Hero's heart Leander lies."*) So, slightly emending the text, he turned a meaningless accepted reading of Juvenal, *"Perditus ac vilis sacci mercator olentis,"* into a characteristically vivid satiric stroke: *"Perditus ac similis sacci mercator olentis"*—the money-chasing merchant, on a stormy voyage, turns as yellow as his bag of saffron. (*"They shook, they stared as white's their shirt: Them it was their poison hurt."*) So, without even an emendation and simply by indicating a new relation between three words of Virgil's, he was able to save Virgil's style in a phrase—*fallax herba veneni*—which had always up to then been read as if it had been written with neither style nor grammar: substituting for "the deceitful plant of poison," "the plant that dissimulates its venom." (*"And bear from hill and valley The daffodil away That dies on Easter day"*; *"Lie long, high snowdrifts in the hedge That will not shower on me"*; *"Snap not from the bitter yew His leaves that live December through."*) Several of his readings, I understand, have been confirmed by the subsequent discovery of manuscripts which Housman had never seen.

To this rescue of the Greek and Roman poets from the negligence of the Middle Ages, from the incompetence and insensitivity of the scholars, A. E. Housman brought an unremitting zeal which may almost be described as a passion. It has been said of the theorems of Newton that they cause the pulse to beat faster as one follows them. But the excitement and satisfaction afforded by the classical commentary of Housman must be unique in the history of scholarship. Even the scraping of the rust from an old coin is too tame an image to convey the experience of pursuing one of his arguments to its climax. It is as if, from the ancient author, so long dumb with his language itself, his very identity blurred or obliterated, the modern classicist were striking a new spark of life—

as if the poet could only find his tongue at the touch across Time of the poet. So far is Housman the scholar a giver of life—yet it is only as re-creator. He is only, after all, again, discovering things that were already there. His findings do not imply a new vision.

It was a queer destiny, and one that cramped him—if one should not say rather that he had cramped himself. (Not to dispute, however, with Housman, who thought that human beings were all but helpless, the problem of natural fate and free will.)

The great work of A. E. Housman's life in the field of classical scholarship was his edition of the five books of Manilius, the publication of which alone extended from 1903 to 1930. We are told in a memoir of Housman by his colleague, Professor A. S. F. Gow of Cambridge, that Housman regarded Manilius as "a facile and frivolous poet, the brightest facet of whose genius was an eminent aptitude for doing sums in verse." And the layman may be disposed to assume that by Housman's time the principal Latin poets had already been covered so completely that there was nobody left except third-rate ones like Manilius. But it turns out from Professor Gow that Housman's real favorite was Propertius, and that he had done a great deal of valuable work on him and had at one time contemplated a complete edition. Professor Gow says that presumably Housman saw in Manilius and Lucan (Lucan he seems also to have despised) "more opportunity than in Propertius of displaying his special gifts, and more hope of approaching finality in the solution of the problems presented," but adds that he "cannot help regretting that he [Housman] abandoned a great and congenial poet on whom so much time had already been lavished."

The elegist of *A Shropshire Lad,* then, deliberately and grimly chose Manilius when his real interest was in Propertius. There is an element of perversity, of self-mortification, in Housman's career all along. (Gow tells how up to the time of his death "he would be found reading every word of books whose insignificance must have been apparent in ten pages, and making remorseless catalogues of their shortcomings.") And his scholarship, great as it is in its way, is poisoned in revenge by the instincts which it seems to be attempting to destroy, so that it radiates more hatred for his opponents than love for the great literature of antiquity. Housman's papers on classical subjects, which shocked the sense of decorum of his colleagues, are painful to the admirers of his poetry. The bitterness here *is* indecent as in his poetry it never is. In a prose, old-fashioned and elaborate, which somewhat resembles Pope's, he will attack the German professors who have committed the unpardonable sin of editing the Latin authors inadequately with sentences that coil and strike like rattlesnakes, or that wrap themselves around their victims and squeeze them to death like boa constrictors. When English fails, he takes to scurrilous Latin. And the whole thing is likely at any moment to give way to some morose observation on the plight of the human race: "To believe that wherever a best *ms* gives possible readings it gives true readings, and that only when it gives impossible readings does it give false readings, is to believe that an incompetent editor is the darling of Providence, which has given its angels charge over him lest at any time his sloth and folly should produce their natural results and incur their appropriate penalty. . . . How the world is managed, and why it was created, I cannot tell; but it is no feather-bed for the repose of sluggards." And not only, he continues, has the notion been imposed that "inert adhesion to one authority is methodical criticism," but "rational criticism has been branded with a term of formal reprobation." "But still there is a hitch. Competent editors exist; and side by side with those who have embraced 'the principles of criticism,' there are those who follow the practice of critics: who possess intellects, and employ them on their work. Consequently their work is better done, and the contrast is mortifying. This is not as it should be. As the wise man dieth, so dieth the fool: why then should we allow them to edit the classics differently? If nature, with flagitious partiality, has given judgment and industry to some men and left other men without them, it is our evident duty to amend her blind caprice; and those who are able and willing to think must be deprived of their unfair advantage by stringent prohibitions. In Association football you must not use your hands, and similarly in textual criticism you must not use your brains. Since we cannot make fools behave like wise men, we will insist that wise men should behave like fools: by these means only can we redress the injustice of nature and anticipate the equality of the grave."

And here is the somber and threatening, the almost Isaian, utterance to which he is moved by the failure of one of the compilers of a German-Latin dictionary to include in the article on *aelurus,* the Latinized Greek word for *cat,* any mention of an instance of its occurrence arrived at by an emendation in Juvenal and believed by Housman to be the first extant: "Everyone can figure to himself the mild inward glow of pleasure and pride which the author of this unlucky article felt while he was writing it and the peace of mind with which he said to himself, when he went to bed that night, 'Well done, thou good and faithful servant.' This is the felicity of the house of bondage, and of the soul which is so fast in prison that it cannot go forth; which commands no outlook on the past or the future, but believes that the fashion of the present, unlike all fashions heretofore, will endure perpetually and that its own flimsy tabernacle of second-hand opinions is a habitation for everlasting."

Even when Housman is saying something positive the emotion is out of proportion to its object: he speaks feverishly, seems unnaturally exalted. Here is a passage on Bentley from the preface to the first volume of his Manilius: *"Lucida tela diei:* these are the words that come into one's mind when one has halted at some stubborn perplexity of reading or interpretation, has witnessed Scaliger and Gronovius and Huetius fumble at it one after another, and then turns to Bentley and sees Bentley strike his finger on the place and say *thou ailest here, and here.* . . . The firm strength and piercing edge and arrowy swiftness of his intellect, his matchless facility and adroitness and resource, were never so triumphant as where defeat seemed sure; and yet it is other virtues that one most admires and welcomes as one turns from the smoky fire of Scaliger's genius to the sky and air of Bentley's: his lucidity, his sanity, his great and simple and straightforward fashion of thought." Transferring Arnold's words for Goethe to Bentley is not perhaps comparing great things with small, but in the substitution for the "physician of the Iron Age" of the physician of mangled texts, there is a narrowing of scope almost comic. The preface to the first book of Manilius, from which the above passage has been quoted, magnificent as it is in its way, has also something monstrous about it.

Yet some acquaintance with the classical work of Housman greatly increases one's estimate of his stature. One encounters an intellectual pride almost Dantesque or Swiftian. "You would be welcome to praise me," he writes, "if you did not praise one another"; and "the reader whose good opinion I desire and have done my utmost to secure is the next Bentley or Scaliger who may chance to occupy himself with Manilius." His arrogance is perhaps never more ferocious than when he is judging himself severely: when a friend who had ventured to suggest the publication of a paper on Swinburne which Housman had read before a college literary society had been told by Housman that he was leaving directions to have it destroyed after his death and had retorted that if the writer really thought it so bad, he would already himself have destroyed it, Housman replied: "I do not think it bad: I think it not good enough for me." And he put on the title page of his edition of Juvenal, *editorum in usum edidit,* to indicate that this feat of erudition—according to his own announcement, unprecedented—was merely intended as a hint to future scholars who might tackle the subject as to how they might accomplish their task in a thoroughgoing fashion.

Is this the spectacle of a great mind crippled? Certainly it is the spectacle of a mind of remarkable penetration and vigor, of uncommon sensibility and intensity, condemning itself to duties which prevent it from rising to its full height. Perhaps it is the case of a man of genius who has never been allowed to come to growth. Housman's anger is tragic like Swift's. He is perhaps more pitiable than Swift, because he has been compelled to suppress himself more completely. Even when Swift had been exiled to Ireland, he was able to take out his fury in crusading against the English. But A. E. Housman, giving up Greek in order to specialize in Latin because he "could not attain to excellence in both," giving up Propertius, who wrote about love, for Manilius, who did not even deal with human beings, turning away from the lives of the Romans to rivet his attention to the difficulties of their texts, can only flatten out small German professors with weapons which would have found fit employment in the hands of a great reformer or a great satirist. He is the hero of *A Grammarian's Funeral*—the man of learning who makes himself impressive through the magnitude, not the importance, of his achievement. After all, there was no need for another Bentley.

It is only in the Latin verses—said to have been called by Murray the best since the ancient world—which Housman prefixed to his Manilius, in his few translations from Latin and Greek, and in his occasional literary essays, that the voice of the Shropshire Lad comes through—that voice which, once sped on its way, so quickly pierced to the hearts and the minds of the whole English-speaking world and which went on vibrating for decades, disburdening hearts with its music that made loss and death and disgrace seem so beautiful, while poor Housman, burdened sorely forever, sat grinding and snarling at his texts. Would he have called back that voice if he could, as he recalled, or tried to recall, so much else? There are moments when his ill humor and his pedantry, his humility which is a perverse kind of pride, almost make us think that he would.

At this point Professor Gow is able to throw some further light on his friend. It seems that Housman had marked the following passage from Colonel Lawrence's *Seven Pillars of Wisdom,* which he had come across in a review:

> There was my craving to be liked—so strong and nervous that never could I open myself friendly to another. The terror of failure in an effort so important made me shrink from trying; besides, there was the standard; for intimacy seemed shameful unless the other could make the perfect reply, in the same language, after the same method, for the same reasons.
>
> There was a craving to be famous; and a horror of being known to like being known. Contempt for my passion for distinction made me refuse every offered honor. I cherished my independence almost as did a Beduin, but my impotence of vision showed me my shape best in painted pictures, and the oblique overheard remarks of others best taught me my created impression. The eagerness to overhear and oversee myself was my assault upon my own inviolate citadel.

Housman had written in the margin, "This is me." Both had been compelled by their extreme sensibility to assume in the presence of their fellows eccentric or repellent masks. Both had been led by extreme ambition to perform exploits which did not do them justice, exploits which their hearts were but half in: Professor Gow says that Housman's prime motive in undertaking his edition of Manilius was the ambition to "build" himself "a monument." And just as Lawrence was always losing the manuscripts of his books, limiting their circulation, making the pretense of suppressing them altogether, so Housman kept his poems out of anthologies, made the gestures of a negative attitude in regard to the reprinting of his other writings, and left instructions that his classical papers, of which Gow says there are something like a hundred, should never be collected in a volume (instructions which it is to be hoped will be disobeyed).

Both were products of the English universities; and it would take an Englishman properly to account for them. But their almost insane attempts to conceal their blazing lights under bushels are recognizable as exaggerations of the Englishman's code of understatement in connection with his achievements and conquests. And both obviously belong to the monastic order of English university ascetics. The company to which Housman refers himself is that of Walter Pater, Lewis Carroll, Edward FitzGerald and Gerald Manley Hopkins—and, earlier, Thomas Gray. Hopkins, converted at Oxford, entered the Jesuit order; Pater and Dodgson stayed on there as dons; FitzGerald and Gray, when they had finished at Cambridge, continued to haunt the place: they remained men of the monastery all their lives. Are their humility, which seems imposed by moral principles, their shyness in relation to the extra-collegiate world, derived from the ages when learning was the possession of pious brotherhoods and shut away between the walls of foundations?

Certainly their failure to develop emotionally is due to that semimonastic training. All seem checked at some early stage of growth, beyond which the sensibility and the intellect—even, in Lawrence's case, the ability to manage men—may crystallize in marvelous forms, but after which there is no natural progress in the experience of human relationships. Their works are among the jewels of English literature rather than among its great springs of life; and Alice and the Shropshire Lad and Marius the Epicurean are all the beings of a looking-glass world, either sexless or with an unreal sex which turns only toward itself in the mirror of art. Isn't the state of mind indicated by Lawrence in the first of the paragraphs quoted above essentially an adolescent one? We are told, in a recent memoir, that Housman used to rail against marriage and childbearing. "My father and my mother," he makes one of his hanged heroes say, "They had a likely son, And I have none."

It would not be true to say of Housman, as it would be of Fitz-Gerald or Gray, that his achievement has been merely to state memorably certain melancholy commonplaces of human existence without any real presentation of that existence as we live it through. There *is* immediate emotional experience in Housman of the same kind that there is in Heine, whom he imitated and to whom he has been compared. But Heine, for all his misfortunes, moves at ease in a larger world. There is in his work an exhilaration of adventure—in travel, in love, in philosophy, in literature, in politics. Doleful though his accents may sometimes be, he always lets in air and light to the mind. But Housman is closed from the beginning. His world has no opening horizons; it is a prison that one can only endure. One can only come the same painful cropper over and over again and draw from it the same bitter moral.

And Housman has managed to grow old without in a sense ever knowing maturity. He has somehow never arrived at the age when the young man decides at last to summon all his resources and try to make something out of this world he has never made.

# Housman

## by John Wain

I have been expecting—but not, so far, seeing—a resurgence of interest in Housman; if not as a poet, then at least as a case-history. After all, he was, in his day, almost alone in facing a problem which is nowadays faced by quite a number of people: the problem of how to combine the two functions of poet and professor. If we read "literary artist of any kind" for "poet," and "academic teacher of any kind" for "professor," we have a situation that is very much of our time; both in England and America, the universities are coming to provide a shelter for writers which saves them from having to be schoolteachers or ad men—though there is still no tendency, in this country at any rate, for a university to employ a poet *because* he is a poet. He gets the job first, in the normal way, and then shyly produces his poems. It is one illustration of the way the universities have taken over some of the social functions of the Church; in the seventeenth century a lot of the best poets were parsons, because the Church was then what the university is today—a large, impersonal, non-profit-making organization, securely established, and able to use men of diverse talents in diverse ways.

However, a modern university teacher is not in the same position as a seventeenth-century clergyman. He has more work to do, for one thing; and, on the whole, harder work. Furthermore, he is under pressures which none of his predecessors knew. When his academic colleagues are not sneering at him for being literary, his literary friends are sneering at him for being academic, and both groups are very good at sneering. Worst of all, he is trying to serve two gods at once, and haunted by the fear that he will, in the end, satisfy neither. As an artist, he needs *luxe, calme, volupté, ordre,* and *beauté,* and all the university can supply him with (perhaps, fortunately) is *ordre* and a limited amount of *calme.* It is not an accident that, until very recent times, no don except Lewis Carroll (and, would one add, Pater?) ever wrote a work of imaginative literature that had enough vitality to keep it alive.

Housman side-stepped these problems, partly by luck and partly by giving in to them. When I say "luck," I mean that his extraordinary talent for emending Latin texts brought him, in early middle life, a Cambridge chair which seems to have involved no very arduous duties. When I say "giving in" I mean that Housman made no attempt to do two things at once. He merely assimilated the poet in him to the professor. The smallness of his output, the narrowness of his range, the elaborate pains he took to safeguard the text from misprints (as if he were one of his own dead authors), are all academic characteristics. So was his inability, or refusal, to develop, to admit any new light, to *move* in any direction.

I must elaborate this last point a little. Housman's major faults as a poet—the things that kept him a *minor* poet—are (*a*) the immature and commonplace nature of his subject-matter, all self-pity and grumbling; (*b*) the lack of any development. Although he wrote poems over a period of some forty years, it is oddly true that if one shuffled them, and had only internal evidence to go by, one would never recover the original order. That is why I feel justified in discussing him among "Victorian" poets, in spite of his going on writing until well into my own lifetime. The last poems he wrote are no different from the first; that is, they exhibit faults (*a*) and (*b*) above.

Now this is such an extraordinary thing—for after all it is human to develop, and we usually do so whether we wish to or not—that one has to ask the reason for it. I have already called it an *academic* characteristic; and, unfortunately, the evidence seems to bear me out. There is something about the academic atmosphere that fosters habit, repetition, getting set in one's ways. Everything is so permanent. Perhaps all institutions do this; certainly the Army and the Church have both been accused of it.

And of course a professor is like a colonel or an archdeacon in one respect: most of his work consists of doing the same thing over and over again. When Housman had finished taking one class through Propertius, there would be another waiting to begin. When he had edited one piece by Manilius, he started on another one just like it.

Now Housman can hardly be blamed for succumbing to this petrification. If it is true that even the strongest minds go down, how could he resist? For his was not, in any broad sense, a strong mind. His stock of ideas was tiny, his human responsiveness, after early life, almost nil; his general intelligence, poor. (Cite *one* interesting remark that Housman made on any general topic.) His getting himself ploughed in Greats was good strategy; it enabled him to claim not to have been trying; and there is no evidence that he would have done well if he *had* tried. Philosophy was obviously alien ground to him. If the tendency of Cambridge was to shut him off from life, it must be said that he collaborated to the full. He spared no pains to turn himself into the solitary, life-resisting, formidable figure of the anecdotes. The banked-up fires exploded in two directions only; his poems, and his savage baiting of other scholars who did not conform to his standards of accuracy.

I have often thought that the bitterness with which Housman attacked his classical colleagues was, to some extent, compensatory. It is a common characteristic of men who have a special, and narrow, gift that they are harshly critical of anyone who tries to compete with them. Housman's gift of emendation was the product partly of industry and partly of the hypersensitive quality of his ear. (Poets are often good at emendation; there is an emendation of Milton's in the received text of the *Bacchae* of Euripides.) It was, in other words, largely a *knack*. He knew a lot of Latin, and he had a knack of making a special use of what he knew. It was a gift, like his poetry. And neither gift had much to do with the ordinary functions of the intelligence. Housman was not a very intelligent man; his poetry proves it. His poetry also proves that he was supremely, if narrowly, gifted.

These remarks may seem merely provoking, but I think they can be proved. After all, a very gifted poet *can* be a stupid man;

his stupidity will keep him a minor poet, but it will not spoil his gift. And a great classical scholar can be stupid too, off his own ground. Bentley, who is usually named as Housman's only superior, has left us detailed proof of his imbecility, in his emendations of *Paradise Lost.* What, then, is the moral?

The moral is, if you are going to be an academic poet, *be stupid.* Dig in, refuse to grow, and cultivate your most specialized talent. Then both sides will respect you. Housman was fantastically over-praised, in his lifetime and since, by his fellow academics, because he offers a justification of the donnish way of life. But for the young writer, employed at a university, he is the *memento mori.* The dead hand of academicism, which kills everything it touches, lay heavily on his exquisite gift. He rejected life, and life certainly had its own back on his poetry, which never gets free of a certain triviality, a certain pettiness and lack of emotional breadth. Even when he re-works a poem by a much better poet, he dares not follow his guide out into the open; I am thinking of that imitation he did of one of the "Lucy" poems; we had better quote the texts:

> A slumber did my spirit seal;
> I had no human fears:
> She seemed a thing that could not feel
> The touch of earthly years.

> No motion has she now, no force;
> She neither hears nor sees;
> Rolled round in earth's diurnal course,
> With rocks, and stones, and trees.

> The night is freezing fast,
> To-morrow comes December;
> And winterfalls of old
> Are with me from the past;
> And chiefly I remember
> How Dick would hate the cold.

> Fall, winter, fall; for he,
> Prompt hand and headpiece clever,
> Has woven a winter robe,

    And made of earth and sea
      His overcoat for ever,
    And wears the turning globe.
                    [*Last Poems,* xx]

Housman has here followed Wordsworth fairly closely; the subject-
matter is identical, except for the change of the dead person's
gender, and the number of stanzas is the same, though the form
is of course varied. Also, each poem brings in two figures; the
dead person, and the "I" through whom the situation is presented. On comparing them more closely, however, the first thing
we become aware of is that Wordsworth has got much more into
his eight lines than Housman has into his twelve; not only more
emotional delicacy and intensity, but actually more in quantity.
The "I" of Housman's poem is static; his function is merely to
say what has happened and to reminisce about past winters and
how Dick hated the cold, in a way that reveals a rather mawkish
feeling for the youth. Wordsworth's "I," on the other hand, is
as much the subject of the poem as the dead girl; whether we
take the first stanza as self-criticism ("I was too complacent, because I was happy in my love for her; I did not think she could
even age, and now she has gone and *died*"), or as a simple statement of a fact ("This is how so great a love makes you feel"), we
are inescapably aware of the "I" as an acting, feeling identity.
Further, since so short a poem needs a certain antithetical balance
of structure to give it the required density, we notice that this
counterpart between his previous "slumber" and *her* present in-
sensibility to motion and force, gives the effect of balancing the
two stanzas against one another. Wordsworth also manages to
communicate, not precisely but unmistakably, that it is *because* of
his lack of awareness that Lucy's death is so great a tragedy; if
he had only been more alive to a natural process such as the passage
of years, he would have valued his time with Lucy differently, and
her pantheistic merging with the earth would not have seemed a
privation, but merely a logical conclusion. The poem nowhere
actually says this, but it is my experience (with students, etc.) that
most readers pick up some such impression.
    If we turn to the Housman immediately afterwards, the weak-

nesses of the lesser poet are thrown into startling relief. The whimsey of the diction ("headpiece," "overcoat," in the same poem as "robe," etc.) by comparison with the truthful simplicity of Wordsworth's; the silly suggestion that it was "clever" of Dick to get into the earth to keep warm, by comparison with the tragic dignity of Wordsworth's pantheism! Even the over-artful stanza form seems vulgar by comparison, as also does the fake pastoralism of naming the boy "Dick," thus lining him up with all the other lads and chaps in Housman's poetry.

Housman alone, of all the poets I have been discussing, had a public that was solidly behind him throughout his writing life; he was uncritically accepted as a genius from the moment he published his first volume, and even today any disparagement of his work is certain to be greeted by a chorus of protests. I don't want to draw any crude moral from the fact that the best of these poets (Tennyson, Browning, Hopkins, Housman) was the one who had least support from the "reading public," and the worst the one who had most; but the reflection should help to calm those who are inclined to panic about the smallness of the public for poetry.

# Jehovah Housman and Satan Housman

## by W. H. Auden

Heaven and Hell. Reason and Instinct. Conscious Mind and Unconscious. Is their hostility a temporary and curable neurosis, due to our particular pattern of culture, or intrinsic in the nature of these faculties? Can man only think when he is frustrated from acting and feeling? Is the intelligent person always the product of some childhood neurosis? Does Life only offer two alternatives: "You shall be happy, healthy, attractive, a good mixer, a good lover and parent, but on condition that you are not overcurious about life. On the other hand you shall be attentive and sensitive, conscious of what is happening round you, but in that case you must not expect to be happy, or successful in love, or at home in any company. There are two worlds and you cannot belong to them both. If you belong to the second of these worlds you will be unhappy because you will always be in love with the first, while at the same time you will despise it. The first world on the other hand will not return your love because it is in its nature to love only itself. Socrates will always fall in love with Alcibiades; Alcibiades will only be a little flattered and rather puzzled"?

To those who are interested in this problem, A. E. Housman is one of the classic case histories. Few men have kept Heaven and Hell so rigidly apart. Jehovah Housman devoted himself to the emendation of texts of no æsthetic value and collected thunderbolts of poisoned invective in notebooks to use when opportunity arose against the slightest intellectual lapses; Satan Housman believed that the essence of poetry was lack of intellectual content.

"Jehovah Housman and Satan Housman" by W. H. Auden. From *New Verse*, No. 28 (January, 1938), pp. 16–17. Copyright 1938 by W. H. Auden. Reprinted by permission of W. H. Auden and Geoffrey Grigson. A review of Laurence Housman's *A.E.H.* (London: Jonathan Cape, 1937).

Jehovah Housman lived the virginal life of a don; Satan Housman thought a good deal about stolen waters and the bed. Jehovah Housman believed that slavery was necessary to support the civilised life; Satan Housman did not accept injustice so lightly.

> But they've pulled the beggar's hat off for the world to see and stare,
> And they're taking him to justice for the colour of his hair.
>
> [*Additional Poems,* xviii]

But they had one common ground upon which they could meet; the grave. Dead texts; dead soldiers; Death the Reconciler, beyond sex and beyond thought. There, and there only, could the two worlds meet.

Mr. Laurence Housman's memoir of his brother records a great many interesting facts from which the reader must construct his own theory of what happened to Housman to cause this division, of why, for instance, he did not work for Greats, and why he did not allow his family to come to see him in those critical years from 1882–1892. But however fascinating such speculations may be, they are of minor importance. What happened to Housman happens in one way or another to most intellectuals, though few exhibit the symptoms in so pure a form.

> The stars have not dealt me the worst they could do:
> My pleasures are plenty, my troubles are two.
> But oh, my two troubles they reave me of rest,
> The brains in my head and the heart in my breast.
>
> Oh grant me the ease that is granted so free,
> The birthright of multitudes, give it to me,
> That relish their victuals and rest on their bed
> With flint in the bosom and guts in the head.
>
> [*Additional Poems,* xvii]

Yes, the two worlds. Perhaps the Socialist State will marry them; perhaps it won't. Perhaps it will always be true that

> *Wer das Tiefste gedacht, liebt das Lebendigste,*
> *Hohe Tugend versteht, wer in die Welt geblickt*
> *Und es neigen die Weisen*
> *Oft am Ende zu Schönem sich.*

[He who has thought deepest, loves that which is most alive; he who has looked into the world understands high virtue; and the wise turn often at the last to beauty. (Hölderlin, "Socrates and Alcibiades")]

Perhaps again the only thing which can bring them together is the exercise of what Christians call Charity, a quality for which, it will be remembered, neither Jehovah nor Satan Housman had much use, but of which perhaps they were both not a little frightened.

# A. E. Housman: A Controversy

### by Cyril Connolly
### (with replies by F. L. Lucas, Martin Cooper,
### L. P. Wilkinson, and John Sparrow)

## I

The obituaries of Professor Housman have given us the picture of a fascinating personality and have made real, to an unscholarly public, the labours of an unrivalled scholar. But in one respect they seem to me misleading, that they all defer to him as a fine lyric poet, the equal of Gray according to some, acclaimed by Sir Walter Raleigh as the greatest living poet according to others. Now there are so few people who care about poetry in England, and fewer still who are critical of it, that one is tempted at first to make no comment. But in case there are some fellow waverers, and in case we can be of small comfort to those whose ideas about poetry are the opposite of Professor Housman's, and whose success also varies inversely to that of the Shropshire Bard, I have made a few notes on his lyrics that may be of use to them.

It is the unanimous verdict of his admirers that Housman is essentially a classical poet. Master of the Latin language, he has introduced into English poetry the economy, the precision, the severity of that terse and lucid tongue. His verses are highly finished, deeply pagan; they stand outside the ordinary current of modern poetry, the inheritors, not of the romantic age, but of the poignancy and stateliness, the lapidary quality of the poems of Catullus,

"A. E. Housman: A Controversy" by Cyril Connolly, with replies by F. L. Lucas, Martin Cooper, L. P. Wilkinson, and John Sparrow. From the *New Statesman*, May 23–June 6, 1936. Copyright 1936 by the *New Statesman*. Reprinted by permission of the authors and the *New Statesman*. This controversy was included by Cyril Connolly in *The Condemned Playground* (London: Routledge, 1945), pp. 47–62.

Horace, and Virgil, or of the flowers of the Greek Anthology. This impression is heightened by the smallness of Professor Housman's output and by the years he devoted to finishing and polishing it, and, not least, by the stern and cryptic hints in the prefaces, with their allusions to profound emotions rigidly controlled, to a creative impulse ruthlessly disciplined and checked. This theory seems to have hoodwinked all his admirers; their awe of Housman as a scholar has blinded them to his imperfections as a poet, just as the pessimism and platonism of Dean Inge have sanctified his opinion on topics which, in other hands, might suggest silly season journalism. The truth is that many of Housman's poems are of a triteness of technique equalled only by the banality of the thought; others are slovenly, and a quantity are derivative—not from the classics, but from Heine, or from popular trends—imperialism, place-nostalgia, games, beer—common to the poetry of his time. *A Shropshire Lad* includes with some poems that are unworthy of Kipling others that are unworthy of Belloc, without the excuse of over-production through economic necessity which those writers might have urged. Horace produced, in the *Odes* and *Carmen Seculare,* a hundred and four poems; Housman, not I think without intention, confined his two volumes to the same number. Yet a moment's silent comparison should settle his position once and for all. To quote single lines, to measure a poet by his mistakes, is sometimes unfair; in the case of a writer with such a minute output it seems justified. Here are a few lines from *A Shropshire Lad,* a book in which, incidentally, the word "lad" (one of the most vapid in the language) occurs sixty-seven times in sixty-three poems.

Each quotation is from a separate poem.

(*a*) Because 'tis fifty years to-night
       That God has saved the Queen.      [i]

(*b*) Clay lies still, but blood's a rover;
       Breath's a ware that will not keep.
       Up, lad: . . .                              [iv]

(*c*) I will go where I am wanted, for the sergeant does not mind;
       He may be sick to see me but he treats me very kind.      [xxxiv]

(*d*) The goal stands up, the keeper
       Stands up to keep the goal.      [xxvii]

(e) And since to look at things in bloom
Fifty springs are little room.    [ii]

(f) You and I must keep from shame
In London streets the Shropshire name;    [xxxvii]

(g) They put arsenic in his meat
And stared aghast to watch him eat;
They poured strychnine in his cup
And shook to see him drink it up.    [lxii]

These are some of the verses that, we are told, could not be entrusted to anthologies because of the author's fears that they would suffer through incorrect punctuation! (a), (b), and (c) suggest barrack-room Kipling, (d) old-boys'-day Newbolt, (e) and (f) are typical of Georgian sham-pastoral, and (g) suggests non-vintage Belloc.

So much for a few of the bad poems. Let us now examine the better ones. There are two themes in Housman: man's mortality, which intensifies for him the beauty of Nature, and man's rebellion against his lot. On his treatment of these themes subsists his reputation for classicism. But his presentation of both is hopelessly romantic and sentimental, the sentiment of his poems, in fact, is that of Omar Khayyám, which perhaps accounts for their popularity; he takes over the pagan concept of death and oblivion as the natural end of life and even as a not inappropriate end of youth, and lards it with a purely Christian self-pity and a romantic indulgence in the pathetic fallacy. By the same treatment his hero becomes a picturesque outlaw, raising his pint-pot in defiance of the laws of God and man, running away to enlist with the tacit approval of his pawky Shropshire scoutmaster, and suitably lamented by him when he makes his final escape from society, on the gallows. In the last few poems it is his own mortality that he mourns, not that of his patrol, but here again his use of rhythm is peculiarly sentimental and artful, as in his metrically morbid experiments in the five-line stanza:

For she and I were long acquainted
And I knew all her ways
[*Last Poems,* xl]

or

> Well went the dances
> At evening to the flute.
>
> [*Last Poems,* xli]

It must be remembered, also, that classical poetry is essentially aristocratic; such writers as Gray or Horace address themselves to their own friends and would be incapable of using Maurice, Terence, and the other rustics as anything but the material for a few general images.

> The boast of heraldry, the pomp of power
> And all that beauty, all that wealth e'er gave,
> Awaits alike the inevitable hour:
> The paths of glory lead but to the grave.

That is classical in spirit.

> Too full already is the grave
> Of fellows that were good and brave
> And died because they were
>
> [*Last Poems,* xxxviii]

is not.

There are about half a dozen important poems of Housman, of which I think only the astronomical one (*Last Poems,* 36) is a complete success. Two were given us at my school to turn into Latin verses.

> Into my heart an air that kills
> From yon far country blows
>
> [*A Shropshire Lad,* xl]

was one, which would suggest to a Roman only a miasma; one has to put it beside "There is a land of pure delight" to realize its imperfection in English, and the other was

> With rue my heart is laden
> For golden friends I had,
> For many a rose-lipt maiden
> And many a lightfoot lad.
>
> By brooks too broad for leaping
> The lightfoot boys are laid;

> The rose-lipt girls are sleeping
> In fields where roses fade.
>
> [*A Shropshire Lad,* liv]

This I have been told is the purest expression in English poetry of the spirit of the Greek Anthology—one of the few things that might actually have been written by a Greek. Yet the first line is Pre-Raphaelite; "golden friends" could not go straight into a classical language, "lightfoot lad" is arch and insipid. The antithesis in the last two lines is obscure. Once again it is a poem in which not a pagan is talking, but someone looking back at paganism from a Christian standpoint, just as the feelings of an animal are not the same as the feelings of an animal as imagined by a human being. The other important verses are in *Last Poems.* There is the bombastic epigram on the army of mercenaries, again with its adolescent anti-God gibe, and the poem which in texture seems most Horatian of all:

> The chestnut casts his flambeaux, and the flowers
> Stream from the hawthorn on the wind away,
> The doors clap to, the pane is blind with showers.
> Pass me the can, lad; there's an end of May.
>
> [*Last Poems,* ix]

The first verse, indeed, except for that plebeian "can," has an authentic Thaliarchus quality—but at once he is off again on his denunciations of the Master Potter—"Whatever brute and blackguard made the world." Even the famous last stanza,

> The troubles of our proud and angry dust
> Are from eternity, and shall not fail.
> Bear them we can, and if we can we must.
> Shoulder the sky, my lad, and drink your ale

suffers from the two "pass the cans" that have preceded it, and from the insincerity of pretending that drinking ale is a stoical gesture identical with shouldering the sky instead of with escaping from it. The poem does, however, reveal Housman at his poetical best—as a first-rate rhetorician. The pity is that he should nearly always have sacrificed rhetoric in quest of simplicity. Unfortunately his criterion of poetry was, as he explained, a tremor in the solar plexus, an organ which is seldom the same in two people, which writes poetry at midnight and burns it at midday, which experiences the sudden chill, the hint of tears, as easily at a bad film as at a good verse. Rhetoric is safer.

*The Waste Land* appeared at the same time as *Last Poems,* and the Phlebas episode may be compared, as something genuinely classical, with them. The fate which Housman's poems deserve, of course, is to be set to music by English composers and sung by English singers, and it has already overtaken them. He will live as long as the B.B.C. Otherwise, by temporarily killing the place-name lyric, his effect was to render more severe and guarded the new poetry of the Pylon school. His own farewell to the Muse reveals him at his weakest, with his peculiar use of "poetical" words:

> To-morrow, more's the pity,
> Away we both must hie,
> To air the ditty,
> And to earth I.
>
> [*Last Poems,* xli]

This is not on a level with Gray: it contains one cliché and two archaisms (*hie* and *ditty*), nor does it bear any resemblance to a classical farewell, such as Horace's:

> *Vivere si recte nescis, decede peritis:*
> *Lusisti satis, edisti satis atque bibisti.*
> *Tempus abire tibi est, ne potum largius aequo*
> *Rideat et pulset lasciva decentius aetas.*

[If you know not how to live aright, make way for those who do. You have played enough, have eaten and drunk enough. 'Tis time to quit the feast, lest, when you have drunk too freely, youth mock and jostle you, playing the wanton with better grace.]

## II [1]

Sir,—Debate about the merits of poetry produces not light, but merely heat. But certain *facts* in Mr. Cyril Connolly's article on Housman seem open to question.

"The unanimous verdict of the Housman admirers is that he

[1] The four letters which follow appeared in *The New Statesman and Nation* in response to the foregoing review.

is essentially a classical poet." It is surely fatal to go on using terms like "classical" and "romantic" without defining which of their many meanings one intends. But if Heine be a "romantic" poet, as most would agree, then so is Housman. He has "classical" qualities, also; but he clearly remains more nearly akin by far to Heine than to Horace. What is Mr. Connolly's evidence for this "unanimous verdict"?

"He takes over the pagan concept of death and oblivion . . . and lards it with a purely Christian self-pity and a romantic indulgence in the pathetic fallacy." Why are we to believe self-pity peculiar to Christians? Has Mr. Connolly never read Homer or Greek tragedy or Theocritus or the Greek Anthology or Lucretius or Virgil or Horace, with all their lamentations? And if "the pathetic fallacy" be a fault, how much of the world's poetry is free from it, from the "lonely-hearted crag" of Aeschylus to the winds that answer Lear?

"Metrically morbid experiments in the five-line stanza"—why is a five-line stanza "morbid"?

"Classical poetry is essentially aristocratic; such writers as Gray or Horace . . . would be incapable of using Maurice, Terence, and the other rustics as anything but the material for a few general images." Yet Homer could call a swineherd "divine" and devote pages to him; a Greek, Theocritus, took shepherds for his heroes and founded European pastoral; and the Greek Anthology is full of "the huts where poor men lie." Why in any case blame Housman for not being "classical"? Is *all* romanticism bad?

"The insincerity of pretending that drinking ale is a stoical gesture identical with shouldering the sky instead of with escaping from it"—why "insincerity"?

> The feather pate of folly
> Bears the falling sky.

Here is no pretence of heroism; it is a commonly observable fact of human psychology.

> To-morrow, more's the pity,
> Away we both must hie,
> To air the ditty,
> And to earth I.

"This," we are told, "is not on a level with Gray; it contains one cliché and two pedantries (*hie* and *ditty*), nor does it bear any resemblance to a classical farewell." Why should it? And if "more's the pity" is a forbidden cliché, are we to understand that no poet must ever use a phrase from ordinary speech? And why is it "pedantic" to call a song a "ditty"? The pedantry may well seem to some to lie elsewhere. In a word, "Why pass an Act of Uniformity against poets?"

F. L. Lucas.

King's College, Cambridge.

[Mr. Lucas read "archaism" as "pedantry."—C. C.]

---

Sir,—As a regular reader of *The New Statesman and Nation* I often get a great deal of pleasure and amusement from Mr. Cyril Connolly's articles. They are *par excellence* the voice of the Opposition; but they have a certain antiseptic quality and act as an effective antidote to our national drug of complacency. In your last week's number, however, I felt that Mr. Connolly had overstepped himself and joined the ranks of the professional denigrators, those often disappointed carpers to whom it is painful to hear praise of anyone or anything. I understand and share Mr. Connolly's objection to the Housman cult; I believe that both Housman and T. E. Lawrence gained false reputations by the persistent silence and mystery with which they surrounded themselves. I agree with Mr. Connolly again when he dismisses the claim of classicism made for Housman's poetry by many of his admirers—though never, so far as I know, by himself. It is only when Mr. Connolly extends his objections to the whole of Housman's work, except "about half a dozen" poems, that I part company with him. Here, surely, the mania for debunking accepted masters has gone too far, and there is an ungenerousness and a pettiness in Mr. Connolly's attack—not rendered less ungenerous or less petty by the moment chosen for its launching—which recalls Yeats' eight lines "On those that hated *The Playboy of the Western World*."

Mr. Connolly chose seven quotations from Housman's most unfortunate poems, lines which in many, but not all, cases not even the poet's greatest admirers would defend, and he analysed these passages as examples of Housman's "triteness and banality" and his essentially unclassical outlook. To deal with the last charge first, I admit that Housman was not a classical poet, but I cannot see that to have been influenced by Heine rather than (or as well as) by Horace or Catullus makes anyone a bad writer. It surely does no more than make those who called him an essentially classical poet bad critics. The charge of "triteness and banality" is linked with that of being under the influence of "the popular trends—imperialism, place-nostalgia, games, beer." Now I will not deny that many poems written under these influences have been bad, nor that some of Housman's in this category are very bad. But the influences themselves, which have been popular in other days besides Housman's, do not always make for bad poetry. Virgil was inspired by imperialism, I suppose, when he wrote the *Aeneid,* and it was place-nostalgia that moved Euripides to write in *Iphigenia in Tauris* the chorus beginning

Ὄρνις, ἃ παρὰ πετρίνας
πόντου δειράδας, ἀλκυών

[Thou bird, who by scaurs o'er the sea-breakers leaning/Ever chantest thy song.]

and prompted Catullus' *"Paene insularum, Sirmio, insularumque."* The Greeks were not unmoved by games, and Pindar's Olympiads do not bear a merely formal title, while the pleasures of drink have inspired almost as many and as good poems—Anacreon and Horace, without thinking—as the pleasures of love. It would have been possible for Mr. Connolly to pick seven unfortunate passages from any poet, however great, and the reason for their badness would in most cases, as in Housman, lie not in their subject-matter, but in a flaw or lapse in the poet himself.

When Mr. Connolly turns to what he calls the "better" poems of Housman, he finds them "romantic and sentimental." Let us grant him that they are often enough romantic; this is surely not a crime in itself. The charge of sentimentality seems to reduce itself to a repetition of the charge of being unclassical. Is not the five-line stanza unclassical rather than "metrically morbid"? And is it a serious criticism of any aspect of a poem except its classicality to say that

> Into my heart an air that kills
> From yon far country blows

—lines worthy of Emily Brontë at her best—"would suggest only a miasma to a Roman"? They suggest something very different to the twentieth-century Englishman, by and for whom they were written; but it is something which at least rests on a background of Christian culture and is therefore strictly unclassical. Mr. Connolly attacks Housman on this same religious issue, and points, as with derision, at his position half-way between Christianity and Paganism. I find it rather perverse to magnify the line

> What God abandoned, these defended

in the "Epitaph on an Army of Mercenaries" into an "adolescent anti-God gibe"; and the line

> Whatever brute and blackguard made the world

in *Last Poems* is surely negatived, as a serious expression of Housman's own feeling, by the lines in a preceding verse—

> May will be fine next year as like as not:
> Oh ay, but then we shall be twenty-four.

Young men of twenty-three must be allowed to feel bitter with the world occasionally (and perhaps Mr. Connolly must be allowed to call them adolescent); the rightness of the line in its context seems unassailable.

The other scholar-poet and pessimist whom Housman resembles in many ways, Giacomo Leopardi, wrote at the age of thirty-five of

> . . . *Il brutto*
> *Poter che, ascoso, a commun danno impera*

—the hideous power which, hidden, orders all things to the common woe, and yet, like Housman, he could never forget or step outside the Christian civilization into which he was born. Many of the greatest European poets have held a position half-way between the two worlds, and it has lent a breadth of sympathy and often a certain pathos to their works. It would be foolish to compare Housman even with Leopardi, to mention no greater names; but it was certainly neither his religious feelings nor his dependence

or independence of classical models which made him a lesser poet
—limited, but within those limitations a master. It would be more
generous at the time of his death to dwell on his mastery rather than
the limits of the field in which he showed it.

Martin Cooper.
Chelsea.

---

Sir,—Mr. Cyril Connolly, in his eccentric note on Housman's
poetry, asserts that "golden friends" could not go straight into
a classical language. Why not? Socrates could exclaim in Plato's
*Phaedrus* (235 E): φίλτατος εἶ καὶ ὡς ἀληθῶς χρυσοῦς, ὦ Φαῖδρε, "you are
a dear, Phaedrus, and golden indeed." And even if this be dis-
counted because their talk has been of golden statues, the word
occurs in the same sense elsewhere in Greek—in Lucian, for
instance, and later in Synesius. But the usage is still more familiar
in Latin. Tibullus (I, 6, 58) refers to Delia's mother as *aurea anus.*
Or take a poet whom Mr. Connolly seems to know; he need only
read as far as the fifth Ode of Horace to find the word applied to
Pyrrha in a well-known passage—*"qui nunc te fruitur credulus
aurea"*—from which Dryden introduced it into English:

> To her hard yoke you must hereafter bow,
> Howe'er she shines all golden to you now.

Housman's use of the word is nearer to the classical than to
Shakespeare's. For the "golden lads and girls" in *Cymbeline* are
gilded primarily with *wealth* as contrasted with the chimney-
sweepers, and elsewhere Shakespeare points the same contrast:

> 'Tis better to be lowly born
> Than wear a golden sorrow.

About Housman's "lads" there is no such suggestion.

L. P. Wilkinson.
King's College, Cambridge.

---

Sir,—Late for the funeral, Mr. Connolly at least had the satisfaction of arriving in time to spit upon the grave before the
mourners had departed. His article on Professor Housman, with
its reference to the "pawky Shropshire scoutmaster" and "his
patrol," appearing when it did, was a brilliant piece of journalistic

opportunism; but, as criticism, it suffered from an evident desire on the writer's part to display his dissent from popular opinion at a time when that display would attract the maximum of attention. This was a pity, because Mr. Connolly's criticism is usually admirably balanced, and a balanced criticism of Housman's verse is to be desired, for his reputation suffers from the indiscriminating adulation of many of his admirers.

In his haste, Mr. Connolly made one or two mistakes, and it is to correct these that I write.

Labouring to prove that the spirit of Housman's verse is different from the "classical" spirit, Mr. Connolly says that classical writers being "essentially aristocratic" would be "incapable of using rustics as anything but the material for a few general images." Has he never read Idyll XIV of Theocritus? Or does he think that no one else has? Does he forget that Virgil was marked for the realism of the dialect he put into the mouths of his peasants? Is he unfamiliar with the gibe *"nostri sic rure loquuntur"*?

Again, Mr. Connolly says that the line "Into my heart an air that kills," "would suggest only a miasma to a Roman." Those who know a great deal more of the classics than either Mr. Connolly or I assure me that this is nonsense.

But it was quite unnecessary for Mr. Connolly to venture thus into the classical field, for no discriminating person will deny for a moment that the spirit of Housman's verse is not classical, but romantic. Space spent (as Mr. Connolly spends it) in declaring that the spirit of "With rue my heart is laden" is alien to that of the Greek Anthology is wasted. Its spirit is utterly different, but the poetry itself is none the worse for that. (I observe, with reference to that particular example, that it is merely pretty, and one of the worst poems that Housman ever wrote; Mr. Connolly with remarkable innocence, or remarkable astuteness, quotes it in full as one of his "half-dozen important poems." Several of Mr. Connolly's other quotations are similarly misleading.)

Housman's verse combined, in a most unusual manner, classical form and romantic feeling. Mr. Connolly might have written a valuable article showing where he thought that Housman fell below his classical models in point of form, and where his feeling lapsed into the merely sentimental.

It is a pity that he left that article to be written by someone with greater knowledge and a more balanced judgment, and wrote instead the article that he did.

JOHN SPARROW.

## III

SIR,—I did not know that in the Sacred Wood of English Literature the poetry of Housman was a ju-ju tree, to touch which is punishable with torture and death. Nor that it was, as my two Wykehamist opponents have not delayed to point out, gross bad taste to find fault with it. The death of any writer is always followed by a revaluation of his work, and the *advocatus diaboli* can surely be allowed a hearing. To suppose that there are degrees of being dead, that after three weeks one cannot pass judgment on an author, and that at some unspecified moment afterwards one can, is too nice an interpretation of the etiquette of the grave. There was nothing in my article that Housman would not have said, with far greater venom, of a living adversary, and nothing in it as unbalanced as the panegyrics which preceded.

> The poems of A. E. Housman will endure as long as English poetry is read, his work as a scholar as long as there are people who wish to appreciate the finest shades of language and the obscurest references in the less-known Latin poets. But Housman was not merely an unrivalled Latin scholar, not merely the author of immortal verse, he was perhaps the most remarkable man among all the distinguished figures of his time.

If Mr. Sparrow, who admits that "Housman's reputation suffers from indiscriminating adulation," can write this, is it in such execrable taste to contradict it?

Mr. Cooper goes on to object to my finding only half a dozen good poems in Housman. Is that so few? There are no more in Collins. In his charge that I blame imperialism, place-nostalgia, games, and beer for Housman's "triteness and banality" and not Housman himself he misunderstands me. Great poetry has been written on those themes, but not between 1896 and 1922. I mentioned them only to show how close Housman was to the poetical

fashions of his time. As to the anti-God lines, I find they betray
something undigested and unassimilated in his work. Mr. Cooper
defends "whatever brute and blackguard made the world" as
being appropriate to young men of twenty-three, but nothing else
in the poem is; we know he was between thirty-six and sixty when
he wrote it, and he should either have brought the diction and
philosophy of the rest of the poem down to it, or matured the line
to suit them. I do not agree that nothing is to be gained by comparing Housman to Leopardi. Leopardi was a classical scholar, a
recluse, and a pessimist, but also one of the supreme poets of all
time; when one compares his laments for his youth or for the
untimely deaths of Silvia and Nerina with Housman's Threnodies
one is exactly able to isolate the element of hurdy-gurdy in the
latter. There is, for instance, the subtlety and fine restraint of the
*Sabato del villaggio* when Leopardi reflects on how much happier
the villagers are on the eve of the fête than they will be on the
fête itself, and compares them to a boy looking forward to the
feast of life. "Do not be sorry that your *festa* is slow in coming—
more I will not say," he concludes—far from the crudities of Ludlow
Fair.

Here I should like to answer Mr. Cooper's last objection, which
is also made by Mr. Lucas. I do not mind anyone standing half-
way between the Christian and pagan worlds, but since the handling
of the pagan concept of life should be a very delicate one, and
since it is a position still capable of giving great artistic results, I
do mind the insincere use Housman made of it, constantly over-
doing the notion of mortality and exaggerating it into a cloying
graveyard poetry and a *succès de larmes*. In the same way I like
the "pathetic fallacy," but, because I like it, I resent Housman's
constant indulgence in it, especially in the form of lamenting that
he will not be there to witness some natural phenomenon, or that,
if he has been there, no one will know.

Mr. Lucas and Mr. Sparrow also object to my point about
Housman and his rustics. I know how Homer, Theocritus, and
Virgil made use of them. Homer is detached from his swineherd,
the shepherds of Virgil and Theocritus are either genuine, or the
poet and his friends playing at being them, not both in the same
poem. Now, in the case of Housman there is an uneasy and variable

relationship; he is not quite sure whether he is a peasant himself; with some his relations are more than friendly, at other times he becomes a distant monitor—or are they all Cambridge professors? I maintain there is a deep confusion here, *"meliusne hic rusticus infans?"* We come once more on one of those unresolved situations, as if Homer were suddenly to say, "You're a better man than I am, Eumaeus," or Virgil to interfere between Alexis and Corydon. It was to try and pin down this shifting social status that I used the image of the scoutmaster and his patrol.

Mr. Lucas and Mr. Cooper both inquire about the five-line stanza. Now, Housman generally wrote in four-lined rhyming stanzas, a metre which he often allowed to lapse into a jingle, for he had not the ear of Mr. Eliot or Mr. Yeats. In one of his earlier and in several of his later poems he added a line to this stanza, using it to impart something particularly bitter and poignant, and having thus three similar open rhymes to each verse.

> O let not men remember
> The soul that God forgot,
> But fetch the county kerchief
> And noose me in the knot,
> And I will rot
> [*Last Poems,* xiv]

is an example. Surely there is something overloaded and over-artful about this stanza, especially when the last line is given such emphasis. I therefore called the extra rhyme metrically morbid. I do not object, either, to poets using contemporary speech, as Mr. Lucas thinks, but I do not feel that "more's the pity," "lief would I," "Ay, lad," or

> Then the world seemed none so bad,
> And I myself a sterling lad;
> And down in lovely muck I've lain,
> Happy till I woke again
> [*A Shropshire Lad,* lxii]

succeed as colloquialisms. "Ditty" and "hie," I think, are rather feeble words. When Mr. Sparrow says that I might have written a valuable article showing where Housman fell below his models instead of leaving it to someone with greater knowledge and judgment, he leaves out the other qualification—a far greater certainty that Housman's poetry is permanently important. Also to say "my friends tell me this is nonsense" is not criticism. I should have preferred to hear from Mr. Sparrow more about Housman and Gray. Speaking of Nature, and Gray and Bentley, he wrote: "to make a third [Professor Housman], she joined the other two." This was a claim I contested; may I hope he will substantiate it?

Mr. Wilkinson's letter I think admirable; I only wish I knew the classics well enough to correct other people with the ferocity such knowledge always permits. I admire his examples, but still timidly contend that they are not quite the same as Housman's more sentimental "for golden friends I had." But I think his point is won. May I ask anyone else who feels like writing a letter to consider first how long it is since they read Housman, and what age they were at the time, for he is a poet who appeals especially to adolescence, and adolescence is a period when one's reaction to a writer is often dictated by what one is looking for, rather than what is there? At least let them read a few consecutive poems over and see if they are as good as they once seemed. I think Housman wrote a certain quantity of admirable rhetorical verse, a few beautiful lyrics, and some lovely occasional lines and stanzas, but I still think there is about him something emotionally vulgar and shallow which is reflected in the monotony of his versification and the poverty of his diction. I think he will always have a place, for his good things, in late Victorian poetry, but I shall continue to maintain that he is greatly overrated.

# Texts from Housman

## by Randall Jarrell

The logic poetry has or pretends to have generally resembles induction more than deduction. Of four possible procedures (dealing entirely with particulars, dealing entirely with generalizations, inferring the relatively general from the relatively particular, and deducing the particular from the more general), the third is very much the most common, and the first and second are limits which "pure" and didactic poetry timidly approach. The fourth is seldom seen. In this essay I am interested in that variety of the third procedure in which the generalizations are implicit. When such generalizations are simple ones, very plainly implied by the particulars of the poem, there will be little tendency to confuse this variety of the third procedure with the first procedure; when they are neither simple nor very plainly implied, the poem will be thought of as "pure" (frequently, "nature") poetry. This is all the more likely to occur since most "pure" poetry is merely that in which the impurity, like the illegitimate child of the story, is "such a little one" that we feel it ought to be disregarded. Of these poems of implicit generalization there is a wide range, extending from the simplest, in which the generalizations are made obvious enough to vex the average reader (some of the "Satires of Circumstance," for instance), to the most complicated, in which they entirely escape his observation ("To the Moon"). The two poems of Housman's which I am about to analyze are more nearly of the type of "To the Moon."

"Texts from Housman" by Randall Jarrell. From the *Kenyon Review*, I (1939), 260–71. Copyright 1939 by *Kenyon Review*, transferred 1967 to Mrs. Randall Jarrell. Reprinted by permission of Mrs. Randall Jarrell and the *Kenyon Review*.

2.

Crossing alone the nighted ferry
With the one coin for fee,
Whom, on the wharf of Lethe waiting,
Count you to find? Not me.

The brisk fond lackey to fetch and carry,
The true, sick-hearted slave,
Expect him not in the just city
And free land of the grave.
[*More Poems,* xxiii]

The first stanza is oddly constructed; it manages to carry over
several more or less unexpressed statements, while the statement it
makes on the surface, grammatically, is arranged so as to make the
reader disregard it completely. Literally, the stanza says: *Whom
do you expect to find waiting for you? Not me.* But the denying
and elliptical *not me* is not an answer to the surface question;
that question is almost rhetorical, and obviously gets a *me;* the *not
me* denies *And I'll satisfy your expectations and be there?*—the
implied corollary of the surface question; and the flippant and
brutal finality of the *not me* implies that the expectations are
foolish. (A belief that can be contradicted so carelessly and completely—by a person in a position to know—is a foolish one.) The
stanza says: *You do expect to find me and ought not to* and *You're
actually such a fool as to count on my being there?* and *So I'll be
there, eh? Not me.*

Some paraphrases of the two stanzas will show how extraordi-
narily much they do mean; they illustrate the quality of poetry
that is almost its most characteristic, compression. These paraphrases are not very imaginative—the reader can find justification
for any statement in the actual words of the poem. (Though not
in any part considered in isolation. The part as part has a misleading look of independence and reality, just as does the word as
word; but it has only that relationship to the larger contexts of
the poem that the words which compose it have to it, and its
significance is similarly controlled and extended by those larger
units of which it is a part. A poem is a sort of onion of contexts,

and you can no more locate any of the important meanings exclusively in a part than you can locate a relation in one of its terms. The significance of a part may be greatly modified or even in extreme cases completely reversed by later and larger parts and by the whole. This will be illustrated in the following discussion: most of the important meanings attached to the first stanza do not exist when the stanza is considered in isolation.) And the paraphrases are not hypertrophied, they do not even begin to be exhaustive.

*Stanza* 1: Do you expect me to wait patiently for you there, just as I have done on earth? expect that, in Hell, after death, things will go on for you just as they do here on earth? that there, after crossing and drinking Lethe and oblivion, I'll still be thinking of human you, still be waiting faithfully there on the wharf for you to arrive, with you still my only interest, with me still your absolutely devoted slave,—just as we are here? Do you really? Do you actually suppose that you yourself, then, will be able to expect it? Even when dead, all alone, on that grim ferry, in the middle of the dark forgetful river, all that's left of your human life one coin, you'll be stupid or inflexible or faithful enough to *count* on (you're sure, are you, so sure that not even a doubt enters your mind?) finding me waiting there? How are we to understand an inflexibility that seems almost incredible? Is it because you're pathetically deluded about love's constancy, my great lasting love for you? (This version makes the *you* sympathetic; but it is unlikely, an unstressed possibility, and the others do not.) Or is it that you're so sure of my complete enslavement that you know death itself can't change it? Or are you so peculiarly stupid that you can't even conceive of any essential change away from your past life and knowledge, even after the death that has destroyed them both? Or is it the general inescapable stupidity of mankind, who can conceive of death only in human and vital terms? (Housman's not giving the reasons, when the reasons must be thought about if the poem is to be understood, forces the reader to make them for himself, and to see that there is a wide range that must be considered. This is one of the most important principles of compression in poetry; these implied foundations or justifications for a statement might be called *bases*.) Are you actually

such a fool as to believe that? So I'll be there? Not me. You're wrong.
There things are really different.

One of the most important elements in the poem is the tone
of the *not me*. Its casualness, finality, and matter-of-fact bluntness
give it almost the effect of slang. It is the crudest of denials. There
is in it a laconic brutality, an imperturbable and almost complacent vigor; it has certainly a sort of contempt. Contempt for
what? Contempt at himself for his faithlessness? contempt at himself for his obsessing weakness—for not being faithless now instead
of then? Or contempt at her, for being bad enough to keep things
as they are, for being stupid enough to imagine that they will be
so always? The tone is both threatening and disgusted. It shivers
between all these qualities like a just-thrown knife. And to what
particular denial does this tone attach? how specific, how general a
one? These are changes a reader can easily ring for himself; but
I hope he will realize their importance. Variations of this formula
of alternative possibilities make up one of the most valuable resources of the poet.

The second stanza is most thoroughly ambiguous; there are
two entirely different levels of meaning for the whole, and most
of the parts exhibit a comparable stratification. I give a word-for-
word analysis:

Do not expect me to be after death what I was alive and human:
the *fond* (1. *foolish;* 2. *loving*—you get the same two meanings in
the synonym *doting*) *brisk* (the normal meanings are favorable: *full
of life, keenly alive or alert, energetic;* but here the context forces
it over into *officious, undignified, solicitous, leaping at your every
word*—there is a pathetic ignoble sense to it here) *lackey* (the most
contemptuous and degrading form of the word *servant:* a servile
follower, a toady) *to fetch and carry* (you thought so poorly of me
that you let me perform nothing but silly menial physical tasks;
thus, our love was nothing but the degrading relationship of
obsequious servant and contemptuous master), *the true* (1. *constant,
loyal, devoted, faithful;* 2. *properly so-called, ideally or typically
such*—the perfectly slavish slave) *sick-hearted* (1. cowardly, dis-
heartened in a weak discouraged ignoble way, as a Spartan would
have said of helots, "These sick-hearted slaves"; 2. sick at heart

at the whole mess, his own helpless subjection. There was a man in one of the sagas who had a bad boil on his foot; when he was asked why he didn't limp and favor it, he replied: "One walks straight while the leg is whole." If the reader imagines this man as a slave he will see sharply the more elevated sense of the phrase *sick-hearted slave*) *slave* (1. the conventional hardly meant sense in which we use it of lovers, as an almost completely dead metaphor; this sense has very little force here; or 2. the literal *slave:* the relation of slave to master is not pleasant, not honorable, is between lovers indecent and horrible, but immensely comprehensive —their love is made even more compulsive and even less favorable). But here I leave the word-by-word analysis for more general comment. I think I hardly need remark on the shock in this treatment, which forces over the conventional unfelt terms into their literal degrading senses; and this shock is amplified by the paradoxical fall through *just city* and *free land* into *the grave*. (Also, the effect of the *lackey—carry* and versification of the first line of the stanza should be noted.)

Let me give first the favorable literal surface sense of *the just city and free land of the grave,* its sense on the level at which you take Housman's Greek underworld convention seriously. The house of Hades is the *just city* for a number of reasons: in it are the three just judges; in it are all the exemplary convicts, from Ixion to the Danaides, simply dripping with justice; here justice is meted equally to the anonymous and rankless dead; there is no corruption here. It is the *free land* because here the king and the slave are equal (though even on the level of death as the Greek underworld, the horrid irony has begun to intrude—Achilles knew, and Housman knows, that it is better to be the slave of a poor farmer than king among the hosts of the dead); because here we are free at last from life; and so on and so on.

But at the deeper level, the *just* fastened to *city*, the *city* fastened to *grave*, have an irony that is thorough. How are we to apply *just* to a place where corruption and nothingness are forced on good and bad, innocent and guilty alike? (From Housman's point of view it might be called mercy, but never justice.) And the *city* is as bad; the cemetery looks like a city of the graves, of the stone rectangular houses—but a city without occupations, citizens, without life: a shell, a blank check that can never be filled out. And can we call a land *free* whose inhabitants cannot move a finger, are compelled as completely as stones? And can we call the little cave, the patch of darkness and pressing earth, the *land* of the grave?

And why are we told to expect him not, the slave, the lackey, in the just city and free land of the grave? Because he is changed now, a citizen of the Greek underworld, engrossed in its games and occupations, the new interests that he has acquired? O no, the change is complete, not from the old interests to new ones, but from any interests to none; do not expect him because he has ceased to exist, he is really, finally different now. It is foolish to expect *anything* of the world after death. But we can expect nothingness; and that is better than this world, the poem is supposed to make us feel; there, even though we are overwhelmed impartially and completely, we shall be free of the evil of this world—a world whose best thing, love, is nothing but injustice and stupidity and slavery. This is why the poet resorts to the ambiguity that permits him to employ the adjectives *just* and *free:* they seem to apply truly on the surface level, and ironically at the other; but in a way they, and certainly the air of reward and luck and approbation that goes with them, apply truly at the second level as well. This is the accusation and condemnation of life that we read so often in Housman: that the grave seems better, we are glad to be in it.

We ought not to forget that this poem is a love-poem by the living "me" of the poem to its equally living "you": *when we are dead things will be different—and I'm glad of it.* It is, considerably sublimated, the formula familiar to such connections: *I wish I were dead;* and it has more than a suspicion of the child's *when I'm dead, then they'll be sorry.* It is an accusation that embodies a very strong statement of the underlying antagonism, the real ambivalence of most such relationships. The condemnation applied to the world for being bad is extended to the *you* for not being better. And these plaints are always pleas; so the poem has an additional force. Certainly this particular-seeming little poem turns out to be general enough: it carries implicit in it attitudes (aggregates of related generalizations) toward love, life, and death.

3.

It nods and curtseys and recovers
When the wind blows above,
The nettle on the graves of lovers
That hanged themselves for love.

The nettle nods, the wind blows over,
The man, he does not move,
The lover of the grave, the lover
That hanged himself for love.
[*A Shropshire Lad,* xvi]

This innocent-looking little nature poem is actually, I think, a general quasi-philosophical piece meant to infect the reader with Housman's own belief about the cause of any action. (I am afraid it is a judgment the reader is likely neither to resist nor recognize.) The nettle and the wind are Housman's specific and usual symbols. Housman's poetry itself is a sort of home-made nettle wine ("Out of a stem that scored the hand/I wrung it in a weary land"); the nettle has one poem entirely to itself, xxxii in *More Poems*. No matter what you sow, only the nettle grows; no matter what happens, it flourishes and remains—"The numberless, the lonely,/The thronger of the land." It peoples cities, it waves above the courts of kings; "And touch it and it stings." Stating what symbols "mean" is a job the poet has properly avoided; but, roughly, the nettle stands for the hurting and inescapable conditions of life, the prosperous (but sympathetically presented and almost admiringly accepted) evil of the universe—"great Necessity," if you are not altogether charmed by it. What the wind is Housman states himself (in "On Wenlock Edge the wood's in trouble"; but it is given the same value in several other poems, notably "The weeping Pleiads wester"): the "tree of man" is never quiet because the wind, "the gale of life," blows through it always.

What I said just before the analysis of the first stanza of "Crossing alone the nighted ferry" is true here too; many of one's remarks about the first stanza of this poem will be plausible or intelligible only in the light of one's consideration of the whole poem. In the first line, *It nods and curtseys and recovers,* there is a shock which grows out of the contrast between this demure performance and its performer, the Housman nettle. The nettle is merely repeating above the grave, compelled by the wind, what the man in the grave did once, when the wind blew through him. So living is (we must take it as being) just a repetition of little meaningless nodding actions, actions that haven't even the virtue of being our own— since the wind forces them out of us; life as the wind makes man as the tree or nettle helpless and determined. This illustrates the general principle that in poetry you make judgments by your own preliminary choice of symbols, and force the reader who accepts the symbols to accept the judgments implicit in them. A symbol, like Bowne's "concept," is a nest of judgments; the reader may accept the symbols, and then be cautious about accepting judgments or generalizations, but the damage is done.

The images in the poem are quite general: "the nettle on the graves of lovers that hanged themselves for love" is not any one nettle, not really any particular at all, but a moderately extensive class. (If Housman were writing a pure poem, a nature poem, he would go about it differently; here the generality is insisted on— any lover, any nettle will do well enough: if you prove something for *any* you prove it for *all*, and Housman is arranging all this as a plausible *any*.) There is of course irony, at several levels, in a nettle's dancing obliviously (*nod* and *curtsey* and *recover* add up to *dance*) on the grave of the dead lover. All flesh is grass; but worse here, because the grass which is the symbol for transitoriness outlasts us. (The reader may say, remembering *The stinging nettle only will still be found to stand:* "But the nettle is a symbol of lasting things to Housman, not of transitory ones." Actually it manages for both here, for the first when considered as a common symbol, for the second when considered as Housman's particular one. But this ambiguity in symbols is frequent; without it they would be much less useful. Take a similar case, *grass:* this year's grass springs up and withers, and is shorter than man; but *grass*, all grass, lasts forever. With people we have different words for the two aspects, *men* and *man*. The whole business of thinking of the transitory grass as just the same more lasting than man—in one form or another, one of the stock poetic subjects—is a beautiful fallacy that goes like this: *Grass*—the year-after-year process—is more lasting than *men;* substituting *man* for *men* and this year's blade for the endless grass, you end by getting a proposition that everybody from Job on down or up has felt, at one time or another, thoroughly satisfactory.) Why a nettle to dance on the grave? Because in English poetry flowers grow on the graves of these lovers who have died for love, to show remembrance; Housman puts the nettle there, for forgetfulness. In the other poems the flower "meant" their love—here the nettle means it. All the nettle's actions emphasize its indifference and removedness. The roses in the ballads were intimately related to the lovers, and entwined themselves above the graves—the nature that surrounded the lovers was thoroughly interested in their game, almost as human as they; the nettle above this grave is alone, inhuman and casual, the representative of a nature indifferent to man.

The fifth and sixth lines of the poem are there mainly to establish this shocking paradox: here is a sessile thing, a plant, that curtseys and nods, while the man, the most thoroughly animate of all beings, cannot even move. Looked at in the usual way this is gloomy and mortifying, and that is the surface force it has here; but looked at in another way, Housman's way, there is a sort of triumph in it: the most absolute that man can know. That is what it is for Housman. Once man was tossed about helplessly and incessantly by the wind that blew through him—now the toughest of all plants is more sensitive, more easily moved than he. In other words, death is better than life, nothing is better than anything. Nor is this a silly adolescent pessimism peculiar to Housman, as so many critics assure you. It is better to be dead than alive, best of all never to have been born—said a poet approvingly advertised as seeing life steadily and seeing it whole; and if I began an anthology of such quotations there it would take me a long time to finish. The attitude is obviously inadequate and just as obviously important.

The triumph here leads beautifully into the poem's final statement: the triumph at being in the grave, one with the grave, prepares us for the fact that it was the grave, not any living thing, that the lover loved, and hanged himself for love of. The statement has some plausibility: hanging yourself for love of someone is entirely silly, so far as any possession or any furthering of your love is concerned, but if you are in love with death, killing yourself is the logical and obvious and only way to consummate your love. For the lover to have killed himself for love of a living thing would have been senseless; but his love for her was only ostensible, concealing—from himself too—the "common wish for death," his real passion for the grave.

But if this holds for this one case; if in committing this most sincere and passionate, most living of all acts (that is, killing yourself for love; nothing else shows so complete a contempt for death and consequences, so absolute a value placed on another living creature), the lover was deceiving himself about his motives, and did it, not for love of anything living, but because of his real love for death; then everybody must do everything for the same reason. (This is a judgment too exaggerated for anyone to expect to get away with, the reader may think; but judgments of life tend to this form—"Vanity, vanity, all is vanity.") For the lover is the perfectly simplified, extreme case. This is what is called a crucial experiment. (It is one of Mill's regular types of induction.) The logic runs: If you can prove that in committing this act—an act about the motives of which the actor is so little likely to be deceived, an act so little likely to have the love of death as his motive—the actor was deceived, and had the love of death as his motive, then you can prove it for any other act the motive of which is more likely to be the love of death, and about the motives of which it is more likely that the actor might be deceived.

But for the conclusion to be true the initial premise must be true, the lover's one motive must have been the wish for death; and Housman has of course not put in even a word of argument for the truth of that premise, he has merely stated it, with the most engaging audacity and dogmatism—has stated it innocently, as a fact obvious as any other of these little natural facts about the wind and the nettle and the cemetery. He has produced it not as a judgment but as a datum, and the sympathetic reader has accepted it as such. He is really treating it as a percept, and percepts have no need for proof, they are neither true nor false, they are just there. If he had tried to prove the truth of the premise he would have convinced only those who already believed in the truth of the conclusion, and those people (i.e., himself) didn't need to be convinced. With the poem as it is, the reader is convinced; or if he objects, the poet can object disingenuously in return, "But you've made the absurd error of taking hypothetical reasoning as categorical. My form is: *If* A, *then* B; I'm not interested in *proving* A. Though, of course, if you decide to remove the *if*, and assert A, then B is asserted also; and A is awfully plausible, isn't it?—just part of the data of the poem; you could hardly reject it, could you?"

Two of the generalizations carried over by this poem—that our actions are motivated by the wish for death, that our ostensible reasons for acts are merely rationalizations, veneers of apparent motive overlying the real levels of motivation—are, in a less sweeping form, psychological or psychoanalytical commonplaces today. But I am not going to hold up Housman's poem as a masterly anticipation of our own discoveries; so far as I can see, Housman was not only uninterested but incapable in such things, and pulled these truths out of his pie not because of wit, but because of the perverse and ingenious obstinacy that pulled just such gloomy judgments out of any pie at all. Here the shock and unlikeliness of what he said were what recommended it to him; and the discovery that these have been mitigated would merely have added to his gloom.

# Alfred Edward Housman

## by Cleanth Brooks

It is tempting to regard A. E. Housman's poetry as classical—in its lucidity, its symmetry, its formal patterning, its laconic bite and edged intensity. Our disposition to do so is encouraged by the fact that Housman was a professor of Latin at Cambridge University and an eminent scholar of the classics. But, as has been frequently observed, Houseman is actually the most romantic of poets, and he himself pointed to thoroughly "romantic" sources for his own poetry in naming "Shakespeare's songs, the Scottish border ballads, and Heine." The essentially romantic nature of his conception of poetry was confirmed in Housman's famous lecture, *The Name and Nature of Poetry.* To a Cambridge that had largely shifted its allegiance and worshipped new gods, Housman proclaimed the old gospel: his summary of the history of English poetry still saw the Romantic revolt as the one far-off, divine event to which, from its first beginnings, the whole creation of English poetry had moved. But Housman's poetry is not only generally and fundamentally romantic: it reflects its particular era, the romanticism of the late nineteenth century. As the late John Peale Bishop once put it: "He is the poet of the end of an age. . . ."

But, of course, this again is not the whole story. Here, on the centenary of the poet's birth, we are concerned with what in his poetry transcends his own time and speaks to us now in the mid-twentieth century. Beyond even that, of course, we are interested in what is truly timeless in Housman's poetry. Perhaps a useful

"Alfred Edward Housman" by Cleanth Brooks. From *Anniversary Lectures Under the Auspices of the Gertrude Clarke Whittall Poetry and Literature Fund* (Washington, D.C.: Library of Congress, 1959), pp. 39–56. Reprinted by permission of Cleanth Brooks and by courtesy of the Library of Congress.

means for realizing this timeless quality is to see what he has in common with some of the writers of our own day.

Two of Housman's constant themes are courage and stoic endurance, and these are themes which are almost obsessive for several of our best contemporary writers. To name only two, there are William Faulkner and Ernest Hemingway. The gap between Housman's Shropshire lads and Hemingway's bullfighters or boxers or big-game hunters may seem shockingly wide, but it is actually less wide than we think. The gap narrows when we place beside Housman's doomed young soldiers the typical Hemingway hero as man-at-arms during the first World War. The idioms used, I grant you, are sharply dissimilar. Hemingway's brilliantly realistic, acrid Midwestern American speech is a whole world away from the faintly archaic, wholly British idiom which is the staple of Housman's lyrics.

> The street sounds to the soldiers' tread,
>     And out we troop to see:
> A single redcoat turns his head,
>     He turns and looks at me . . . .
>
> What thoughts at heart have you and I
>     We cannot stop to tell;
> But dead or living, drunk or dry,
>     Soldier, I wish you well.
>                   [*A Shropshire Lad,* xxii]

But, I repeat: beneath these surface differences, the situation, the stance taken, the attitude assumed, may not be different at all. Indeed, Hemingway, it seems to me, can throw a great deal of light upon Housman and, though I venture this more hesitantly, Housman may throw a good deal of light on Hemingway.

A good place to start is with one of Housman's finest short poems, but a poem too little known, his "Epitaph on an Army of Mercenaries":

> These, in the day when heaven was falling,
>     The hour when earth's foundations fled,
> Followed their mercenary calling
>     And took their wages and are dead.

> Their shoulders held the sky suspended;
> They stood, and earth's foundations stay;
> What God abandoned, these defended,
> And saved the sum of things for pay.

It has been said that this brilliant little poem commemorates the small British professional army which heroically took its beating in the early days of the first World War, but which, in spite of terrible losses, managed to slow down and finally to stop the German advance, and so held the Channel ports. I dare say this may be true, so far as concerns the specific occasion. But the poem has a universal application. It does not celebrate merely the tough professional soldier who fights for his country, not because of some high-sounding ideal but because fighting is his profession—because that is the way he makes his living. The poem surely celebrates all of those hard-bitten realists who are often regarded as mere materialists and yet who frequently outdo the perfervid idealists and self-conscious defenders of the right.

If this is what the poem celebrates, then we are not so far from Hemingway's characteristic stance after all. One remembers, in *A Farewell to Arms*, Lt. Henry's disgust for the great value terms which, for him and his comrades, had become pretentious and empty and therefore lying.

> There were many words that you could not stand to hear and finally only the names of places had dignity. . . . Abstract words such as glory, honor, courage . . . were obscene beside the concrete names of villages, the numbers of roads, the names of rivers, the numbers of regiments and the dates.

But can one really be hired to die? Do Housman's "mercenaries" save the sum of things, as the poet asserts that they do, "for pay"? Isn't there a concealed idealism after all, despite the poet's refusal to allow anything more than the materialistic reason? Of course there is, and this, I suppose, is the point that the poem is making: that the courage to stand and die rather than to run away usually comes from something like *esprit de corps* or professional pride or even from a kind of instinctive manliness rather than from adherence to the conventional rubrics of patriotism and duty. But if this is what Housman's poem implies, then we are indeed in the general realm of Hemingway's fiction, for the mercenaries' gesture is completely consonant with the Hemingway ethos. The Hemingway hero, like Housman's, faces the insoluble "troubles of our proud and angry dust," and in his own way subscribes to the sentiment that

> Bear them we can, and if we can we must.
> Shoulder the sky, my lad, and drink your ale.
> [*Last Poems,* ix]

Of course, it must be added that the drink of the Hemingway hero is more likely to be *grappa* or brandy or seven-to-one martinis.

But Hemingway can show what is *wrong* with a Housman poem just as effectively as he can show what is right. Consider a well-known poem by Housman which I think has to be set down as a failure:

> Could man be drunk for ever
> With liquor, love, or fights,
> Lief should I rouse at morning
> And lief lie down of nights.
>
> But men at whiles are sober
> And think by fits and starts,
> And if they think, they fasten
> Their hands upon their hearts.
> [*Last Poems,* x]

These tough lads who avoid a contemplation of the essential horror of life by keeping the senses occupied with liquor and lechery and fighting are obviously in the same plight as those that we find in *The Sun Also Rises.* Jake, the hero of that fine and sober book, is in spite of himself sober at times, and thinks by fits and starts. But in this case, Hemingway has all the advantage. We can believe in the toughness of his hero and also in his pathos, for both are presented realistically and convincingly. Jake Barnes is never made to fasten his hand upon his heart, and it is this theatrical gesture, so out of keeping with these lusty, brawling, hard-drinking young men, that lets Housman's little poem collapse. The failure does not stem from the fact that the poem falsifies the typical Hemingway situation; it fails because it is inconsistent with its own premises. It is not that the gesture is foreign to Hemingway's Nick Adams: it is a gesture which could not occur in the Shropshire pub of the 1890's. But of course in justice to Housman, Hemingway has his failures too. *Across the River and into the Trees* sentimentalizes the heroic gesture into its own kind of theatricality.

I do not mean to press unduly the Hemingway-Housman analogy. I shall be principally concerned with those qualities that make the finest of Housman's poetry perdurable. But I think that the comparison with Hemingway can be extremely useful in opening up to a contemporary audience the problems which Housman faced and the characteristic failures and characteristic successes which he achieves. In both authors, so dissimilar in so many ways, there is a fairly narrow ambit of interests. The same theme and the same kind of character occur over and over. There is the danger of monotony, the danger of repetition. It seems sometimes to a reader that Housman has only one poem to write, which he writes and rewrites tirelessly, though oftentimes with very brilliant and beautiful variations. With the general narrowness of the ambit there is, as we have seen, the possibility of sentimentality. In general there is a serious problem of tone. The poem must not seem arch or cute. It must achieve its intensity while making use of understatement or laconicism. The close-lipped courage and the stoic endurance must elicit an intense sympathetic response and yet the hero, from the very terms of the situation, is forbidden to cry out or make any direct appeal for our sympathy.

This is the general problem that besets the presentation of the Hemingway hero: he is the tough guy who because of his very toughmindedness sees into the nature of reality and indeed is more sensitive to the tears of things than are those soft and blurred sensibilities whose very fuzziness of response insulates them against the tragic aspects of reality. Yet Housman is a poet who elects to work within a tiny lyric form, barred from the factuality and massively detailed sense of the world which a writer of fiction like Hemingway rightfully has at his disposal.

Let us see how Housman manages the matter in a tiny lyric, which after years of reading remains one of my favorites, a poem entitled "Eight O'Clock."

He stood, and heard the steeple
  Sprinkle the quarters on the morning town.
One, two, three, four, to market-place and people
  It tossed them down.

Strapped, noosed, nighing his hour,
  He stood and counted them and cursed his luck;
And then the clock collected in the tower
  Its strength, and struck.

We learn in the poem almost nothing about the condemned man. We are never told what his crime was. The poem does no more than give us the last half minute of his life. But how brilliantly that half minute is evoked, and with it some sense of his incorrigible spirit as he waits for the clock's stroke which announces the hour of his execution. Everything in the poem cooperates to dramatize the experience. In the last moments of this man's life, time takes on a monstrously heightened quality. The clock, I take it, is one which sounds a musical phrase for each of the quarter hours and finally, at the hour, after the little tune has been completed, the number of the hour is hammered out with separate strokes. The musical phrases, then, are the "quarters" which he hears the steeple "Sprinkle . . . on the morning town." By the way, an earlier draft of the poem is preserved in one of the notebooks possessed by the Library of Congress—notebooks which the Library owns through the generous gift of Mrs. Gertrude Clarke Whittall. The notebook draft reads:

One, two, three, four, on jail and square and people
  They dingled down.

Housman's second thoughts are a brilliant improvement. One does not need the mention of the jail. Suspense requires that the reason for the man's intent listening should not be divulged until we come to the second stanza. Contrast requires too that the "morning town," as it is called in the first stanza, be simply presented as a crowded market-place down to which the steeple clock almost gaily "tosses" its chiming quarters.

But with the second stanza, now that we know that the listener is strapped and noosed, the clock, though it continues to dominate the scene, changes character and collects itself to strike the prisoner

himself. True, the eighth stroke will not be launched vindictively
at the prisoner. It will only signal to the hangman the moment to
pull the trap. But by a brilliant telescoping, the clock, the recorder
and instrument of time, becomes itself the destroyer:

> And then the clock collected in the tower
> Its strength, and struck.

Time is, with Housman, always the enemy. Housman's Shropshire
lad characteristically views the window pane, "blind with showers"
and grudgingly checks off one day of his brief springtime that is
ruined. Or he speaks to a loved one urgently

> Now—for a breath I tarry
> Nor yet disperse apart.
> [*A Shropshire Lad,* xxxiii]

One of Housman's finest poems turns not upon reference to a
clock but to a calendar. The speaker faces the advent of the first
winter month and faces it with a heavy heart.

> The night is freezing fast,
> To-morrow comes December;
> And winterfalls of old
> Are with me from the past;
> And chiefly I remember
> How Dick would hate the cold.

Dick, the friend who is mentioned almost casually in the last line,
is of course the occasion for the poem, and as we shall see in the
next stanza, it is the first fall of snow upon Dick's grave that becomes the matter of the poem. But Dick, his friend observes with a
kind of wry humor, has outwitted winter.

> Fall, winter, fall; for he,
> Prompt hand and headpiece clever,
> Has woven a winter robe,
> And made of earth and sea
> His overcoat for ever,
> And wears the turning globe.
> [*Last Poems,* xx]

Housman has been very daring here. The metaphor with which the
poem ends is as bizarre and witty as one of John Donne's. For the

speaker insists that the earth has not swallowed up Dick but that the dead man has wrapped the earth about himself "And wears the turning globe." For a poet so Victorian in his tastes as Housman was, and a poet generally so inimical to witty conceits—in his famous lecture on poetry Housman will hardly allow the seventeenth-century metaphysicals the name of poets—his conceit of Dick's wearing the globe is very curious indeed. But the bold figure works. The suggestion of schoolboy slang, "prompt hand and headpiece clever," help to prepare for it, and something of extravagance is needed if the poem is not to dissolve into a kind of too pure and direct pathos. But what makes the last lines work is Housman's audacity in using the commonplace and matter-of-fact word "overcoat." He has already called it a "winter robe," and now if he were to name it a "cloak" or a "toga" or even a "garment," the poem would close on a kind of strained embarrassment. But *overcoat* here is triumphantly right. It represents the brilliant handling of tone which is to be found in nearly all of Housman's successful poems. Dick, with his "headpiece clever," the man never at a loss, has finally outwitted the cold, which he always used to hate. This at least is the way in which one might imagine Dick's accounting for the situation: it is a gay piece of schoolboy extravagance and the jest, because it is characteristic of the dead youth, actually renders the sense of grief not less but more intense. There is not a trace of sentimentality.

Sentimentality is a failure of tone. The emotion becomes mawkish and self-regarding. We feel that the poet himself has been taken in by his own sentiment, responds excessively, and expects us to respond with him in excess of what the situation calls for. And so the writer who, like Housman, insists so uniformly upon the pathos of loss, upon the imminence of death, and upon the grim and loveless blackness to come, must be adept at handling the matter of tone.

Housman's great successes (as well as his disastrous failures) are to be accounted for in terms of tone. It does not matter that Housman never himself employs the term. *We* need it, nevertheless, in order to deal with Housman's poetry: for control of tone is the difference between the shrill and falsetto and the quiet but resonant utterance; it is the difference between the merely arch and self-consciously cute and the full-timbred irony; it is the difference between the sentimental and the responsibly mature utterance. Housman's characteristic fault is a slipping off into sentimentality. (One may observe in passing that this is also Hemingway's characteristic fault.) Conversely, Housman's triumphs nearly always involve a brilliant handling of tone—often a startling shift in tone—in which the matter of the poem is suddenly seen in a new perspective.

"The night is freezing fast" exhibits the kind of tonal shift of which I am speaking. "The Immortal Part" will furnish an even clearer example. In this poem, the speaker perversely insists that the immortal part of man is his skeleton—not the spirit, not the soul—but the most earthy, the most nearly mineral part of his body. The bones will endure long after the "dust of thoughts" has at last been laid and the flesh itself has become dust.

The device on which the poem is built is the grumbling complaint of the bones. The speaker begins by telling us that he can hear his bones counting the days of their servitude and predicting the day of their deliverance in which the flesh will fall away from them and leave them free and unfettered. Housman allows to the bones a certain lugubrious eloquence.

> "Wanderers eastward, wanderers west,
> Know you why you cannot rest?
> 'Tis that every mother's son
> Travails with a skeleton.

The reference to "wanderers" makes one suppose that "travails" is spelled "travels," but in fact the word is "travails"; and this suggestion of the travail of childbirth is developed fully in the next two stanzas:

> "Lie down in the bed of dust;
> Bear the fruit that bear you must;
> Bring the eternal seed to light,
> And morn is all the same as night.

> "Rest you so from trouble sore,
> Fear the heat o' the sun no more,
> Nor the snowing winter wild,
> Now you labour not with child.

> "Empty vessel, garment cast,
> We that wore you long shall last.

—Another night, another day."
So my bones within me say.

The colloquy of the bones is brilliant. But can the brilliance be indefinitely sustained? After nine stanzas, there is every danger of monotony. What climatic threat is there left for the bones to utter? And if there is none, how end the poem?

What Housman does is to introduce a brilliant shift in tone. The man answers back:

> Therefore they shall do my will
> To-day while I am master still,
> And flesh and soul, now both are strong,
> Shall hale the sullen slaves along,
>
> Before this fire of sense decay,
> This smoke of thought blow clean away,
> And leave with ancient night alone
> The stedfast and enduring bone.

But this defiance of the bones implies in fact a conviction of the truth of their ultimate triumph. Indeed, the "I" who speaks concedes the bones' eventual victory, and furthermore the last four lines of his speech of defiance simply turn into an echo of the chant of the bones. But the tone of the poem has shifted: the conscious sentient being has refused to collapse before the certain onslaught of time. The human spirit is given its due. The worst has been faced and faced down, though not denied.

Housman's use of a shift in tone is so important in his poetry generally that I should like to exhibit still another instance—one of Housman's finest, that which he employs in "Bredon Hill."

The lovers on many a Sunday morning on Bredon Hill have listened to the church bells ringing out through the valleys.

> In summertime on Bredon
> The bells they sound so clear;
> Round both the shires they ring them
> In steeples far and near,
> A happy noise to hear.
>
> Here of a Sunday morning
> My love and I would lie,

> And see the coloured counties,
> And hear the larks so high
> About us in the sky.

In their own happiness the lovers would put words to the sound
of the bells:

> The bells would ring to call her
> In valleys miles away:
> "Come all to church, good people;
> Good people, come and pray."
> But here my love would stay.

> And I would turn and answer
> Among the springing thyme,
> "Oh, peal upon our wedding,
> And we will hear the chime,
> And come to church in time."

But his sweetheart comes to church before their time.

> But when the snows at Christmas
> On Bredon top were strown,
> My love rose up so early
> And stole out unbeknown
> And went to church alone.

> They tolled the one bell only,
> Groom there was none to see,
> The mourners followed after,
> And so to church went she,
> And would not wait for me.

This last stanza, as the notebooks preserved in this Library reveal,
gave Housman great trouble. He made at least five attempts to
get the phrasing right. I hope that it is not too irreverent of me
to suggest that he never did get it precisely right. I cannot help
resenting the line "The mourners followed after"—not because it
is not true—presumably there were mourners—but because it is
unnecessary—we do not need to be *told* in so many words that the
girl died. Moreover, the direct reference to her death works against
the indirect presentation of it through the poem's basic metaphor
—which treats the funeral as if it were a marriage, in which the

lover is betrayed by his sweetheart who jilts him and steals away
to church to be wed to another.

> And so to church went she,
> And would not wait for me—

not *could* not wait, but *would* not wait, as if her failure to wait for
him were a matter of her own volition.

But whether or not I am right in thinking that Housman's "explaining his metaphor" is a slight blemish in the sixth stanza, how
brilliantly the poem recovers in the seventh, and is brought to an
ending that is beautifully right! I think that you can "hear" the shift
in tone as I read this last stanza:

> The bells they sound on Bredon,
> And still the steeples hum.
> "Come all to church, good people,"—
> Oh, noisy bells, be dumb;
> I hear you, I will come.

The note of exasperation—the irritated outburst against the noise
of the bells—is a powerful, if indirect way, of voicing the speaker's
sense of loss. All come to death; he will come to the churchyard too;
but now that his sweetheart has been stolen from him, what does it
matter *when* he comes. The bells whose sound was once a happy
noise to hear have become a needless and distracting noisiness. The
lover shuts them up as he might the disturbing prattle of a child:

> Oh, noisy bells, be dumb;
> I hear you, I will come.

One of Housman's surest triumphs of tone is the first poem of
*A Shropshire Lad,* the poem simply entitled "1887." The year 1887
was that of Queen Victoria's Jubilee. The village is celebrating the
fiftieth year of her accession to the throne. The beacons have been
lighted and in the village pub they are singing "God Save the
Queen."

> From Clee to heaven the beacon burns,
> The shires have seen it plain,
> From north and south the sign returns
> And beacons burn again.

> Look left, look right, the hills are bright,
> The dales are light between,
> Because 'tis fifty years to-night
> That God has saved the Queen.

But after the light dancing measures and the flickering alliteration of the opening lines, line eight brings us down with a solid bump. "God save the Queen" is a ritualized phrase. One invokes God's favor. One recommends the sovereign to His mercy. But one does not bring the prayerful imperative down into the dust and sweat of ordinary syntax by turning it into the present perfect of an ordinary work-a-day English verb:

> Because 'tis fifty years to-night
> That God has saved the Queen.

It is as if a piece of ritual furniture were suddenly put to some common use: we get a comparable shock.

I shall have more to say of this device in a moment: suffice it to observe at this point that notice has been served that this will be no ordinary Jubilee tribute. And it is not. For the speaker goes on in the stanzas that follow to talk about the absentees on this occasion, the boys who had been abroad on the Queen's business, who did not come home.

> Now, when the flame they watch not towers
> About the soil they trod,
> Lads, we'll remember friends of ours
> Who shared the work with God.

Again, with the last line there is a shock: God has saved the Queen, but He has required the services—or at least has chosen to make use of the services—of human helpers. And some of these have proved to be expendable. The irony is as edged as a knife—and yet it is a quiet and unforced irony; for the statement "Who shared the work with God" is perfectly consonant with the stated premises. For if the defeat of the Queen's enemies is to be attributed ultimately to God, the humbler means, the British infantrymen who have stood off her enemies, have had a share, even if only a humble share, in God's work. But many of the Shropshire lads who went into the armies of the Queen have not returned.

> To skies that knit their heartstrings right,
> To fields that bred them brave,
> The saviours come not home to-night:
> Themselves they could not save.

Here the irony achieves a sort of climax, for the last lines echo the passage in the Gospels in which Christ, hanging on the cross, is taunted with the words: "Others he saved; himself he cannot save." To apply the words associated with the Crucified to the dead soldiers is audacious, but again the words are perfectly applicable, quite simply and literally fitting the case of the absent soldiers. Indeed, a reader who failed to catch the Biblical allusion would not feel that the lines were forced or strained. For soldiers, who must necessarily risk losing their own lives in order to save others, are often to be found in such a plight: Others they saved, "Themselves they could not save."

With the fifth stanza, the poem moves away from the local scene. The speaker lets his imagination wander over the far places of the earth where the dead soldiers now lie.

> It dawns in Asia, tombstones show
> And Shropshire names are read;
> And the Nile spills his overflow
> Beside the Severn's dead.

> We pledge in peace by farm and town
> The Queen they served in war,
> And fire the beacons up and down
> The land they perished for.

We need this expansion of view and we need a momentary rest from the irony that has closed so powerfully stanzas two, three, and four. But after this shift of perspective and alteration of tone, we are returned once more to the Jubilee occasion. The lads of the Fifty-third Regiment—those who did come back, that is—join in the celebration.

> "God save the Queen" we living sing,
> From height to height 'tis heard;
> And with the rest your voices ring,
> Lads of the Fifty-third.

> Oh, God will save her, fear you not:
> Be you the men you've been,
> Get you the sons your fathers got,
> And God will save the Queen.

It is a powerful ending of a brilliant poem. Anyone can feel that. But it may be worth examining a little further the speaker's final attitude. Is the poem anti-royalist? Anti-religious? More specifically, is the man who speaks the poem contemptuous of the lads of the Fifty-third because they naively sing "God save the Queen" and do not realize that it is they who have had to do the dirty work themselves?

As a matter of fact, Housman's own views on the ending of his poem are on record. Frank Harris, in his *Latest Contemporary Portraits,* tells of a talk with Housman about this poem. He writes:

> I recited the last verse as if it had been bitter sarcasm which in all sincerity I had taken it for and I went on: "It stirs my blood to find an Englishman so free of the insensate snobbishness that corrupts all true values here. I remember telling Kipling once that when he mixed his patriotism with snobbery it became disgusting to me; and here you have poked fun at the whole thing and made splendid mockery of it."
>
> To my astonishment, Housman replied sharply: "I never intended to poke fun, as you call it, at patriotism, and I can find nothing in the sentiment to make mockery of: I meant it sincerely; if Englishmen breed as good men as their fathers, then God will save their Queen." His own words seemed to have excited him for he added precisely but with anger: "I can only reject and resent your—your truculent praise."

Housman's angry outburst might seem to settle the matter. But does it? It may dispose of Harris's attempt to read a "bitter sarcasm" into the last stanza. But even Housman's own word for it will hardly smooth the irony out of this poem.

> Lads, we'll remember friends of ours
> Who shared the work with God.

> The saviours come not home to-night:
> Themselves they could not save.

These passages simply defy an innocently literal reading; and in view of Housman's frequently expressed scepticism about the existence of God, the last lines of the poem likewise defy a literal reading.

In angrily rejecting Frank Harris's bitter sarcasm, Housman over-corrected the error. If one reads the entire account printed by Harris, it is easy enough to see what happened. Harris and a pair of his friends had got to talking about Housman's poetry, and one of them proposed that they look the poet up at King's College, London, where he was teaching, and take him to lunch. They called, introduced themselves, and fairly swept him along to lunch with them. This was not the sort of thing that Housman, a shy and fastidious man, would take to, and Frank Harris, with his breezy confidence and his trace of vulgarity, was exactly the sort of man that Housman would abominate. Harris makes it quite plain that no rapport had been established, the conversation had been forced and difficult throughout the luncheon. Resentments of a more pervasive kind and a general antagonism burst forth in Housman's explosion over the meaning of his poem.

We are back, then, once more with the problem of tone. Is it possible to describe the tone of this poem without misrepresenting it on the one hand as a heavy sarcasm and without, on the other hand, falsifying its evident irony? I think that it is possible.

The key to the poet's attitude is to be found in a line of the poem upon which we have already commented:

> Because 'tis fifty years to-night
> That God has saved the Queen.

There, as we remarked, a ritualistic phrase, a pious sentiment, a patriotic cliché is suddenly taken seriously and is made to work in a normal English sentence. It is as shocking as if a bishop suddenly used his crozier like a shepherd's crook to lay hold upon a live sheep.

But to consider soberly the implications of the phrase that is bandied about so thoughtlessly on this jubilant occasion—to reflect upon what is involved in the prayer "God save the Queen"—does not necessarily involve mockery of the Queen or the young men who have helped save her. Housman's protest here is well taken.

His consideration of the cliché, however, does involve a realistic appraisal of the issues and a penetration beneath patriotic shows and appearances. The speaker clearly admires the lads of the Fifty-third but his angle of vision is different from theirs. What they accept naively and uncritically, he sees in its full complexity and ambiguity. But his attitude is not cynical and it is consonant with genuine patriotism. The irony that it contains is a mature and responsible irony whose focus is never blurred. The closing stanza, with its quiet insistence that God will save the Queen but with its conjoined insistence on the all important proviso that they shall get them the sons their fathers got dramatizes the speaker's attitude to a nicety.

A little while ago, I called Housman a romantic poet, a late romantic. If I have emphasized Housman the ironist, it is because I think his irony is important and that its presence does not make him the less a romanticist. But a more obvious aspect of his romanticism may be his treatment of nature.

Many of the poems—and not only those of *A Shropshire Lad*—are given a pastoral setting. The English countryside is everywhere in Housman's poetry. A typical appearance is revealed in the charming lyric which is printed on the back of your programs.[1] To see the cherry in blossom is one of the delights of the year, and how few years there are vouchsafed us in which to see it. Time is the enemy of delight and yet the cherry tree is the product of time. The very description of the springtime beauty is ominous: if "hung with snow" is a way of stressing the unbelievable whiteness of the blossoms, the phrase also hints of winter and the death to come.

But Housman's view of nature looks forward to our time rather than back to that of Wordsworth. If nature is lovely and offers man delight, she does not offer him solace or sustain him as Wordsworth was solaced and sustained. For between Wordsworth and Housman there interpose themselves Darwin and Huxley and Tindall—the whole achievement of Victorian science. The effect of this impact of science is not, of course, to make Housman love nature less: one could argue that it has rendered nature for him more poignantly beautiful. But his attitude toward nature is not

[1] *A Shropshire Lad* ii, printed on the program for Mr. Brooks's lecture, March 26, 1959.

that of the early Romantics and we must take into account this altered attitude if we are to understand his poems.

In this general connection allow me to remark, by the way, that we have had in our day the revival—though it has gone largely unnoticed—of a very fine nature poetry. This nature poetry reveals the somewhat altered perspective of the twentieth century—as is natural and inevitable. But the delight in the rich qualities of the natural scene is extraordinary. Let me extend the term *poetry* to include some of our finest prose fiction. Look at the rendering of nature—to be found, say, in Hemingway and Faulkner. There is a loving attention to detail and faithful evocation of the quality of a scene. The natural world is reflected with beautiful delicacy and even radiance in the fishing episode in Hemingway's *The Sun Also Rises,* or in the hunting scenes of Faulkner's "The Bear." This latter story concludes with what can only be described as a great hymn to nature. If keeping in mind such nature poetry as this, we remember also the characteristic depiction of nature by poets like Thomas Hardy or Robert Frost, we may begin to realize that the twentieth century, in spite of industrialization and the growth of world cities, has indeed produced a rich nature poetry.

Our immensely increased knowledge of nature has not destroyed her charm. Even the so-called scientific neutralization of nature has not done that—not at least for many of our poets. But it has altered their attitudes toward her and it has tended to stress man's sense of his alienation from nature. (Of course, even this sense of alienation is not strictly "modern"—I find it, for example, in Keats' "Ode to a Nightingale.") But the fact of alienation tends to be determinative for the modern nature poet. The poems of Robert Frost testify again and again to the elemental attraction of nature of which man is a part, but Frost never yields to the delusion that man can slip through the invisible barrier to merge himself into nature. The speaker of the poem in every case remembers his manhood and ruefully or with a half-serious jest or with a stoic brusqueness puts down the temptation. When the falling leaves of autumn beckon to Frost's "leaf-treader" to come with them in their descent to death, the man acknowledges the "fugitive in his heart" that wants to respond to the leaves' "invitation to grief," but finally, with a small boy's impudence, he shrugs off the impulse:

But it was no reason I had to go because they had to go
So up my foot to keep on top of another year of snow.

Again, the traveler in "Stopping by Woods on a Snowy Evening" pauses and as he enjoys the beauty of the lovely scene, feels the attraction of nature:

The woods are lovely, dark and deep . . .

But he has promises to keep and it is significant that he drives on. Or again, the man who comes upon the site of the burned farmhouse and abandoned barn is struck by the melancholy of the scene. The very birds who haunt the scene seem to be mourning. But the observer knows better, though

One had to be versed in country things
Not to believe the phoebes wept.

But he *is* versed in country things, and in spite of the temptation to feel that nature sympathizes with man, he knows that she does not. However melancholy the birds may sound to him, they are simply singing out of the fullness of their own activity; they know nothing and care nothing for man's sorrow.

Frost's treatment of nature can help us to understand Housman's, particularly that revealed in what is in some respects Housman's finest poem, with a comment on which I mean to close this lecture. But I am not, of course, so absurd as to suggest that the attitudes of Frost and Housman are identical; and in any case, the poetic strategies of these two fine poets differ in a dozen ways. They speak in different idioms, different intonations. But the resemblance is worth pointing out in order to stress an element of the modern in Housman that we may easily overlook.

Housman expressed his characteristic attitude toward nature in the beautiful poem numbered xl in *Last Poems,* his farewell to nature. The matter of the poem is the speaker's resignation of his mistress Nature to another. The resignation is forced; he does not willingly relinquish her. He has possessed her too completely to feel that she is less than a part of himself and his appetite for her is not cloyed. At this moment of conscious relinquishment, nature has never been more compellingly the enchantress.

> Tell me not here, it needs not saying,
> What tune the enchantress plays
> In aftermaths of soft September
> Or under blanching mays,
> For she and I were long acquainted
> And I knew all her ways.

How thorough is his knowledge of her ways is quietly but convincingly made good in the second and third stanzas.

> On russet floors, by waters idle,
> The pine lets fall its cone;
> The cuckoo shouts all day at nothing
> In leafy dells alone;
> And traveller's joy beguiles in autumn
> Hearts that have lost their own.

> On acres of the seeded grasses
> The changing burnish heaves;
> Or marshalled under moons of harvest
> Stand still all night the sheaves;
> Or beeches strip in storms for winter
> And stain the wind with leaves.

These beautiful stanzas do more than create a series of scenes from nature. They insinuate the speaker's claim to his possession of nature through an intimate knowledge of her ways. Each of the vignettes suggests the secret life of nature revealed to a rapt and solitary observer: the tap of the falling pine cone, audible only because the scene is hushed and breathless; the shouts of the solitary cuckoo, who seems to be calling to no other bird and not even to a human listener but with cheerful idiocy shouting "at nothing"; the flower called "traveller's joy" in the autumn sunshine silently extending to the joyless wayfarer its grace of self, the namesake of joy.

The "changing burnish" on the "acres of the seeded grasses," I take to be the shimmer of light that one sees play upon a hayfield in late summer when the wind heaves and ripples the long grass stems to catch the light. You who have seen it will know that "burnish" is not too extravagant a term, for the grass sometimes

shimmers as if it were metallic. The wind that heaves the grass is
a fitful wind of late summer. That which strips the beech trees
of their leaves is a late autumn gale. But the third scene portrayed
in this stanza—

> Or marshalled under moons of harvest
> Stand still all night the sheaves—

is windless: that is the point, I take it, of the statement that under
the harvest moon the sheaves "Stand *still* all night." The secret life
of nature is thus depicted through all weathers and throughout
the round of the seasons. All of it has been observed by the speaker,
all of it has been made his own possession through knowledge and
is held now in memory. But the various scenes of the changing year
are but the magic spells woven by the one enchantress.

The fourth stanza stresses his claim to possession. The first line
rings the changes upon the word "possess" and the very last word
of the stanza, the emphatic closing rime word, is "mine." But the
action of the stanza is a relinquishment of his claims. The speaker
conjures the companion to whom he speaks the poem to

> Possess, as I possessed a season,
>   The countries I resign,
> Where over elmy plains the highway
>   Would mount the hills and shine,
> And full of shade the pillared forest
>   Would murmur and be mine.

His claim to possession is based upon a shared experience, a secret
knowledge, the kind of bond that unites two lovers who feel that
they belong to each other. But in this instance, the beloved is nature; and nature is not one to recognize any lover's claim to possession.

> For nature, heartless, witless nature—

Nature is not only the fickle mistress, she is the idiot mistress,
having no more mind than heart.

> For nature, heartless, witless nature,
>   Will neither care nor know
> What stranger's feet may find the meadow
>   And trespass there and go,

> Nor ask amid the dews of morning
> If they are mine or no.

Nature, for all her attractiveness to man, is supremely indifferent to him. This is the bedrock fact upon which the poem comes to rest, but if the fact constitutes a primal irony, it is accepted in this poem without rancor or any fierce bitterness. The very charm of nature is the way in which she can give herself freely to all of us who will strenuously try to claim her. And moreover, if nature, in this last stanza, is heartless and witless, she is still as freshly beautiful as the morning. Notice how concretely Housman says this in the closing lines. Nature spreads her dewy meadow as virginally fresh for the imprint of the feet of the trespasser as for those of the old lover who would like to believe that he alone possessed her.

The attitude toward nature here is not Wordsworth's confident trust that "Nature never did betray/The heart that loved her." Yet the poem may be said to illustrate the Wordsworthian formula

> How exquisitely the individual Mind . . .
> . . . to the external World
> Is fitted: —and how exquisitely, too— . . .
> The external World is fitted to the Mind.

True, it is Housman's mind, not Wordsworth's, that is fitted to the landscape here described; but the exquisite fitting is there just the same—so much so that the nature that Housman depicts seems to answer at every point the sensitive and melancholy mind that perceives it, and in its turn implies in its aloof and beautifully closed order the loneliness and austerity of the mind of its observer.

Housman's feet no longer print the dew of his favorite English meadow. What he predicted in the poem has obviously come to pass. The ageless enchantress nature spreads her blandishments now for other men—for us, if we care to respond. But it ought to be noted that Housman has himself responded with an enchantment of his own: I mean the poem itself. The poem matches the immortality of nature with its own kind of immortality—the immortality of art. For, if nature, changeless through all the vicissitudes of change, is unweariedly the same, so also the experience that Housman has dramatized for us here may be endlessly repeated and is eternally recapturable. *Ars longa, vita brevis. We* may trespass into the poet's ancient dominion, see and possess as the poet himself "possessed a season" the woods and fields of Shropshire or of Cambridgeshire. But in participating in his *poem* we will possess more: we will possess his hard-won knowledge of the meaning of possession. Through the poem we shall come to know more deeply what our relation to nature is and what we as men are. Our feet, then, that "trespass" on the poet's ancient dominion, in the magical world of his poem, commit no trespass. His footprints become our own; we stand in his shoes; we share in his experience, which has been treasured up and given a life beyond life. That is what art can do. That is why we must always feel a deep gratitude to the poet. That is why we celebrate Alfred Edward Housman's one hundredth birthday this evening.

# Round About
# A Poem of
# Housman's

## by Richard Wilbur

In the spring of 1944 my division was withdrawn from action and assigned to a rest area not far from Naples. Once we had pitched our tents, painted our tent-pegs white, cleaned and polished our equipment, and generally recovered the garrison virtues, we were allowed to make occasional excursions, in groups of one truckload, to nearby points of interest. I remember best our trip to Pompeii. One reason why I remember it so clearly is that, on the day of our visit, Vesuvius began its worst eruption in many decades. Our six-by-six truck approached Pompeii through a fine, steady fall of whitish flakes, and set us down in a square already carpeted with ash. Some of our party, not caring for archeology, headed directly for the bars and other comforts of the modern city; but the rest of us thought it more seemly to begin, at least, with a look at the ruins. We found a displaced Greek woman who offered to be our guide, and she took us through the greater part of the excavations, pointing out the wall paintings, deciphering inscriptions, explaining the water system—until at last, just as we reached the Greek Forum, there was a sudden darkening of the air, a thickening in the fall of ashes, and she took fright and left us.

We found our way back to the modern city and established ourselves in a bar, sitting near the window so that we could watch for the return of our truck. The street was now full of natives evacuating the place, wading through the ashes under the usual clumsy burdens of refugees. Sitting there with a brandy bottle and watching such a scene, we felt something like the final tableau of *Idiot's Delight.* There were jokes about how we had better look smart and sit straight, since we might have to hold our poses for centuries. And one bookish soldier said that he had never felt so close to Pliny the Elder.

Before we had exhausted that vein of nervous humor, the truck arrived, and our scattered party emerged or was extricated from all the bars and dives of the vicinity. Climbing over the tailgate, most of us had some trophy or memento to show or show around: one had a bottle of Marsala, another a bottle of grappa; one had an album of colored views of the ruins; another drew from that breast-pocket which is supposed to carry a bullet-proof New Testament a packet of French postcards. And then there were cameos from Naples, and salamis, and pure silk placemats marked *Ricordo d'Italia.* When everything had been shown and assessed, one slightly drunken soldier leaned forward on his bench and said, "All right, boys, now you look at *this.*" He held out his fist, opened it, and there on his palm stood a small, good replica of the famous sculpture of the wolf, nursing Romulus and Remus.

"How *about* that?" he said. "Man, ain't that the dirtiest gotdamn statue you ever saw?"

I don't tell that in ridicule of the soldier who said it. He had been a good farmer in East Texas, and he was a good soldier in Italy; his talk had more verve, rhythm, and invention in it—more poetry in it—than one usually hears in the talk of cultured people; and I would not call him inferior, as a man, to the soldier who happened to know that Pliny the Elder was done in by Vesuvius. I tell the story because, in this hopeful democracy of ours, in which the most unpromising are coerced into a system of free public education, we must often remind ourselves that the art public is not coextensive with the population, or even with the voting population. Any poet would feel justified in referring to Romulus and Remus and the wolf—one could hardly find a classical allusion more safely commonplace; and yet there really are millions of Americans who would not understand the reference, and who really might, if they saw the Wolf of the Capitol, mistake it for a dirty statue. We must stubbornly remember this whenever polemicists began to strike the Whitman note, and to ask for a poetry at once serious and universally understandable.

A young Japanese woman told me recently of a parlor game which she and her friends had often played: fragmentary quotations from haiku are written on slips of paper; the slips of paper are put into a box; and then each player draws in his turn, reads out the fragment, and attempts to say the complete seventeen-syllable poem from memory. When cultured young Japanese play such a game as that, they are drawing on a detailed acquaintance with a vast haiku literature reaching back more than seven hundred years. And this acquaintance has to do with far more than subject matter. Haiku literature is, for instance, full of plum blossoms; and in order to see the uniqueness of a fragment having to do with plum blossoms one would have to possess not only a sense of the total history of that motif in Japanese verse, but also an intimate familiarity with the norms of diction, the strategies of suggestion and the modes of feeling which belong to the haiku convention and to its great practitioners. It goes without saying that any modern Japanese poet who writes a haiku can expect his best readers to grasp his every echo, variation, or nuance.

It is both good and bad that for American poets and their clientele there exists no such distinct, subtle, and narrow tradition. Our cultural and literary traditions are longer and far more inclusive than the Japanese, but they shape our lives far less decidedly and are subject to perpetual revision. A professor planning the reading list for a freshman Humanities course scratches his head and wonders whether St. Augustine's conception of history is in any way relevant to our own; one critic decides that our present sense of the past can do without Milton and Shelley, while another discovers that the main line of poetic tradition does, after all, lead through Alexander Pope. Similarly, our poets have shifting and rival conceptions of what the "tradition" is, and this leads in practice to a constant renewal, modification, and blending of conventions. What's good about this situation is that our poetry is not conventionally inhibited from coping with modern life as it comes; the modern poem is an adaptable machine that can run on any fuel whatever. The obvious disadvantage is that our unstable sense of literary tradition, and our dissolving multiplicity of conventions, makes it hard for the educated person not a devotee of poetry to develop *tact*.

A tactful person is one who understands not merely what is said, but also what is meant. In a spring issue of the *New Republic*, a correspondent described the melancholy experience of exposing a class of engineers to a well-known four-line poem by Ogden Nash— the one that goes

> Candy
> Is dandy,
> But liquor
> Is quicker.[1]

As I recall, the article said that only one student in the lot recognized that poem as humor. The others either had no response or took it to be a straight-faced admonitory poem about obesity, blood sugar, or some such thing. Now, it is true that contemporary poets, encouraged by the critical rediscovery of the seriousness of wit, have done much to confound the distinction between light verse and serious poetry. Think how light Robert Frost can be, even in a quite serious poem; and think how often Phyllis McGinley trespasses on the serious. Still, it is a terrible failure of tact to read Mr. Nash's poem with a long face. The little jingly lines, the essentially comic rhymes, and the slangy diction combine to require that we place it within the convention of light verse. From a certainty as to the convention we derive a certainty as to tone, and when we know the tone we know what the subject must be: Mr. Nash is writing about strategies of seduction, a topic on which Americans incline to be coy, and his leaving the subject unstated is equivalent to a wink and a dig in the ribs.

Even in poems where the subject is fully stated, there is a world of difference between what is said and what is meant, and this I should like to prove by a brief absurd example. There is a charming popular song called "Paper Moon," the first eight bars of which go as follows:

---

[1] Reprinted by permission of Curtis Brown, Ltd., and J. M. Dent & Sons, Ltd. Copyright 1930 by Ogden Nash. Renewal copyright © 1957 by Ogden Nash.

> Say, it's only a paper moon
> Sailing over a cardboard sea
> But it wouldn't be make believe
> If you believed in me.[2]

I want now to juxtapose those lines with a passage from Matthew Arnold's "Dover Beach." That poem begins, as you'll remember,

> The sea is calm tonight,
> The tide is full, the moon lies fair
> Upon the straits . . .

and then it proceeds toward this climactic passage:

> Ah, love, let us be true
> To one another! for the world, which seems
> To lie before us like a land of dreams,
> So various, so beautiful, so new,
> Hath really neither joy, nor love, nor light,
> Nor certitude, nor peace, nor help for pain.

It would be possible, I submit, to compose a one-sentence paraphrase which would do for both "Paper Moon" and "Dover Beach." It might go something like this: "The lover begs his beloved to cleave to him, and thus alleviate through human love his painful sense of the meaninglessness of the modern world, here symbolized by the false beauty of the moon." What I have just done is scandalous, of course; but I hope you will agree that it proves something. It proves that if we consider statement only, and work upon it with the disfiguring tool of paraphrase, a frisky pop-song and a tragic poem can be made to seem identical. From this one can see how much of the meaning of any poem resides in its sound, its pacing, its diction, its literary references, its convention—in all those things which we must apprehend by tact.

One of my favorite poems of A. E. Housman is called "Epitaph on an Army of Mercenaries," and because it is a soluble problem in tact I want to discuss it here. Let me say it to you a first time in a fairly flat voice, so as to stress by *lack* of stress the necessity, at certain points, of making crucial decisions as to tone:

[2] Reprinted by permission of Warner Bros.-Seven Arts, Inc., and Anne-Rachel Music Corporation. Copyright 1933 by Harms, Inc.

These, in the day when heaven was falling,
    The hour when earth's foundations fled,
Followed their mercenary calling
    And took their wages and are dead.

Their shoulders held the sky suspended;
    They stood, and earth's foundations stay;
What God abandoned, these defended,
    And saved the sum of things for pay.

Perhaps the main decision to be made is, how to say those last two words, "for pay." Should they be spoken in a weary drawl? Should they be spoken matter-of-factly? Or should they be spat out defiantly, as if one were saying "Of *course* they did it for pay; what did you expect?" Two or three years ago, I happened to mention Housman's poem to a distinguished author who is usually right about things, and he spoke very ill of it. He found distasteful what he called its easy and sweeping cynicism, and he thought it no better, except in technique, than the more juvenile pessimistic verses of Stephen Crane. For him, the gist of the poem was this: "What a stinking world this is, in which what we call civilization must be preserved by the blood of miserable hirelings." And for him, that last line was to be said in a tone of wholesale scorn:

And saved the *sum of things* for *pay*.

I couldn't accept that way of taking the poem, even though at the time I was unprepared to argue against it; and so I persisted in saying Housman's lines to myself, in my own way, while walking or driving or waiting for trains. Then one day I came upon an excellent essay by Cleanth Brooks [see p. 62], which supported my notion of the poem and expressed its sense and tone far better than I could have done. Mr. Brooks likened Housman's Shropshire lads, so many of whom are soldiers, to those Hemingway heroes who do the brave thing not out of a high idealism but out of stoic courage and a commitment to some personal or professional code. Seen in this manner, Housman's mercenaries—his professional soldiers, that is— are not cynically conceived; rather their poet is praising them for doing what they had engaged to do, for doing what had to be done, and for doing it without a lot of lofty talk. If we understand the poem so, it is not hard to see what tones and emphases are called for:

> *These,* in the day when heaven was falling,
> The hour when earth's foundations fled,
> Followed their mercenary calling
> And took their wages and are dead.
>
> *Their* shoulders held the sky suspended;
> *They stood,* and earth's foundations stay;
> What God abandoned, *these defended,*
> And saved the sum of things for pay.

That is how I would read it, and I suspect that Mr. Brooks would concur. But now suppose that the distinguished author who thought the poem wholly cynical should not be satisfied. Suppose he should say, "Mr. Brooks' interpretation is very enhancing, and makes the poem far less cheaply sardonic; but unfortunately Mr. Brooks is being more creative than critical, and the poem is really just what I said it was."

There are a number of arguments I might venture in reply, and one would be this: Housman was a great classical scholar, and would have been particularly well acquainted with the convention of the military epitaph. His title refers us, in fact, to such poems as Simonides wrote in honor of the Spartans who fell at Thermopylae, or the Athenians who fought at the Isthmus. Those poems are celebratory in character, and so is Housman's. The sound and movement of Housman's poem accord, moreover, with the mood of plain solemnity which the convention demands. The tetrameter, which inclines by its nature to skip a bit, and which we have already encountered in "Oh, it's only a paper moon," is slowed down here to the pace of a dead-march. The rhetorical balancing of line against line, and half-line against half-line, the frequency of grammatical stops, and the even placement of strong beats, make a deliberate movement inescapable; and this deliberate movement releases the full and powerful sonority which Housman intends. It is not the music of sardony.

The distinguished author might come back at me here, saying something like this: "No doubt you've named the right convention, but what you forget is that there are *mock*-versions of every convention, including this one. While Housman's mock-use of the military epitaph is not broadly comic but wryly subtle, it does employ the basic trick of high burlesque. Just as Pope, in his mock-epic *The Rape of the Lock,* adopts the tone and matter of Milton or Homer only to deflate them, so Housman sets his solemn, sonorous poem to leaking with the word 'mercenary,' and in the last line lets the air out completely. The poem is thus a gesture of total repudiation, a specimen of indiscriminate romantic irony, and it's what we might expect from the poet who counsels us to 'endure an hour and see injustice done,' who refers to God as 'whatever brute and blackguard made the world,' and who disposes of this life by crying, 'Oh, why did I awake? When shall I sleep again?' "

From now on I am going to play to win, and I shall not allow the distinguished author any further rebuttals. The answer to what he said just now is this: while Housman may maintain that "heaven and earth ail from the prime foundation," he consistently honors those who face up manfully to a bad world; and especially he honors the common soldier who, without having any fancy reasons for doing so, draws his mercenary "thirteen pence a day" and fights and dies. We find this soldier in such poems as "Lancer," or "Grenadier," and Housman always says to him,

> dead or living, drunk or dry,
> Soldier, I wish you well.
> [*A Shropshire Lad,* xxii]

The mercenaries of the poem I've been discussing are enlisted from all these other soldier-poems, and though their deaths exemplify the world's evil, Housman stresses not that but the shining of their courage in the general darkness.

The poem is not a mock-version of the military epitaph; however, the distinguished author was right in feeling that Housman's poem is not so free of irony as, for instance, William Collins' eighteenth-century ode, "How sleep the brave. . . ." These eight short lines do, in fact, carry a huge freight of irony, most of it implicit in a system of subtle echoes and allusions; but none of the irony is at the expense of the mercenaries, and all of it defends them against slight and detraction.

If one lets the eye travel over Housman's lines, looking for echo or allusion, it is probably line 4 which first arrests the attention:

And took their wages and are dead.

This puts one in mind of St. Paul's Epistle to the Romans, Chapter VI, where the Apostle declares that "the wages of sin is death." The implication of this echo is that paid professional soldiers are sinful and unrighteous persons, damned souls who have forfeited the gift of eternal life. That is certainly not Housman's view, even if one makes allowance for ironic exaggeration; and so we are forced to try and imagine a sort of person whose view it might be. The sort of person we're after is, of course, self-righteous, idealistic, and convinced of his moral superiority to those common fellows who fight, not for high and noble reasons, but because fighting is their job. Doubtless you've heard regulars of the American army subjected to just that kind of spiritual snobbery, and one readily finds analogies in other departments of life: think of the way professional politicians are contemned by our higher-minded citizens, while shiny-faced amateurs are prized for their wholesome incapacity. Spiritual snobs are unattractive persons under any circumstances, but they appear to especial disadvantage in Housman's poem. After all, they and their civilization were saved by the mercenaries—or professionals—who did their fighting for them, and that fact makes their scorn seem both ungrateful and hypocritical.

Housman's echo of St. Paul, then, leads us to imagine a class of people who look down on Tommy Atkins, and it also prompts us to defend Tommy Atkins against their unjust disdain. Let me turn now to some other echoes, to a number of Miltonic reverberations which are scattered throughout the poem. They all derive from some ten lines of the Sixth Book of *Paradise Lost*. That is the book about the war in heaven, wherein the good angels and the rebel angels fight two great and inconclusive engagements, after which the Messiah enters and single-handedly drives the rebels over the wall of heaven. It is probably not irrelevant to mention that the ruling idea of Book VI, the idea which all the action illustrates, is that might derives from right, and that righteousness therefore must prevail. Here is a passage which comes at the end of the second battle, when the good and bad angels are throwing mountains at each other:

> . . . horrid confusion heapt
> Upon confusion rose: and now all Heav'n
> Had gone to wrack, with ruin overspread,
> Had not th' Almighty Father where he sits
> Shrin'd in his Sanctuary of Heav'n secure,
> Consulting on the sum of things, foreseen
> This tumult, and permitted all, advis'd (668 ff.).

*The sum of things* means here the entire universe, including heaven and hell, and God is about to save the sum of things by sending his son against the rebel angels. Otherwise heaven might fall, and earth's foundations might flee. When the Messiah drives Satan and his forces over heaven's edge, and they begin their nine-day fall into hell, Milton gives us another passage which Housman has echoed:

> Hell heard the unsufferable noise, Hell saw
> Heav'n ruining from Heav'n, and would have fled
> Affrighted; but strict Fate had cast too deep
> Her dark foundations, and too fast had bound (867 ff.).

It's quite plain that Housman is reminding his reader of Milton, and in particular of these two passages from Book VI, in which we find "the sum of things," fleeing foundations, and heaven in peril of falling. The ticklish question now is, how much of Milton should we put into Housman's poem; how detailed a comparison should we draw between the war in Milton's heaven and the battle in which Housman's mercenaries died? Should we, for instance, compare Housman's sacrificial mercenaries, whose deaths have preserved the sum of things, to the Son of God who won the war in heaven and later died on earth to save mankind? Housman is quite capable of implying such a comparison. In his poem "The Carpenter's Son," Christ is a Shropshire lad who dies on the gallows because he would not "leave ill alone." And in the poem "1887," Housman says this of the soldiers who have helped God save the Queen by dying in battle:

> To skies that knit their heartstrings right,
> To fields that bred them brave,
> The saviours come not home to-night:
> Themselves they could not save.
>
> [*A Shropshire Lad,* i]

As Mr. Brooks points out in his essay, those last lines "echo the passage in the Gospels in which Christ, hanging on the cross, is taunted with the words: 'Others he saved; himself he cannot save.' " It appears, then, that in his "Epitaph on an Army of Mercenaries" Housman may be bestowing on his soldiers the ultimate commendation; he may be saying that their sacrifice, in its courage and in the scope of its consequences, was Christlike. For the rest, I should say that Housman's Miltonic allusions have a clear derogatory purpose, and that their function is once again to mock those who feel superior to the soldiers whom the poet wishes to praise. Housman mocks those who feel that they are on the side of the angels, that their enemies are devils, that God is their property and will defend the right, that heaven and earth depend upon their ascendancy and the prevalence of their lofty mores, yet who count in fact not on God or on themselves but on the courage of mercenaries whom they despise.

These smug people, whom the poem nowhere mentions but everywhere rebukes, are covertly attacked again in line five through an allusion to the eleventh labor of Heracles. In that enterprise, Heracles was out to secure the golden apples of the Hesperides, and he applied for the help of Atlas, the giant who supports the heavens on his shoulders. Atlas agreed to go and get the apples, if Heracles would temporarily take over his burden. When Atlas returned, he noticed that Heracles was supporting the heavens very capably, and it occurred to him that Heracles might well continue in the assignment. Had Heracles not then thought of a good stratagem, and tricked Atlas into reassuming the weight of the skies, he would have been the victim of the greatest buck-passing trick on record. What Housman is saying by way of this allusion is that the battle of his poem was won not on the playing fields of Eton but in the pastures of Shropshire, and that the Etonians, and the other pillars of the established order, transferred their burden in this case to the

lowly professional army. Once we recognize Housman's reference,
we can see again the extent of his esteem for the so-called mercenaries: he compares them to the great Heracles. And once we perceive
that line five has to do with buck-passing, with the transference of
a burden, we know where to place the emphasis. It should fall on
the first word:

> *Their* shoulders held the sky suspended.

It was *they,* the mercenaries, and not the presumptive upholders of
the right, who saved the day.

It seems to me that quite enough allusions have now been
found; there may be others, but if so we don't need them for purposes of understanding. Nor, I think, do we need to consider the
possible fiscal overtones of the words "saved" and "sum." It's true
that in conjunction with the words "wages" and "pay," the phrase
"saved the sum" has a slight clink of money in it, and one could
probably think up an appropriate meaning for such a play on
words. But readers and critics must be careful not to be cleverer
than necessary; and there is no greater obtuseness than to treat
all poets as Metaphysicals, and to insist on discovering puns which
are not likely to be there.

What I've been trying to illustrate, no doubt too exhaustively,
is how a reader might employ tact in arriving at a sure sense of an
eight-line poem. Probably I've gone wrong here or there: I'm afraid,
for one thing, that I've made the poem seem more English and
less universal than it is. But I hope at any rate to have considered
some of the things which need considering: the convention of the
poem; the use of the convention; the sound, pace, and tone of the
poem; its consistency with the author's attitudes and techniques in
other poems; and the implicit argument of its allusions or echoes.
Let me read it a last time:

> These, in the day when heaven was falling,
>   The hour when earth's foundations fled,
> Followed their mercenary calling
>   And took their wages and are dead.
>
> Their shoulders held the sky suspended;
>   They stood, and earth's foundations stay;

> What God abandoned, these defended,
> And saved the sum of things for pay.

Karl Shapiro has lately published in *Poetry* magazine a prose outburst with which I greatly sympathize and yet thoroughly disagree. I won't aim to answer it as a whole, because as he himself says it is too inconsistent to constitute a clear target. You can, within limits, argue with a wild man; wild men are simple; but there's no arguing with a subtle and reasonable man who is bent on being wild. Let me, however, quote one passage from Mr. Shapiro which bears on what I've been saying. He objects to the fact that in our country

> the only poetry that is recognized is the poetry that repeats the past, that is referential. It relates back to books, to other poetry, to names in the encyclopaedia. It is the poetry of the history-inhibited mind only, and as such it is meaningless to people who lack the training to read it. The Little Magazine, the avant-gardist, the culture academician base the esthetic experience on education. Whereas poetry needs not education or culture but the open perceptions of the healthy human organism.

Mr. Shapiro and I agree that a poem which refers to Romulus and Remus and the wolf will be meaningless, in part at least, to those who lack the training to read it. I disagree, however, with Mr. Shapiro's determination to hound that wolf out of poetry, to abolish the literary and historical past, to confine us to the modern city and declare the ruins off-limits. It would not be worth it to make poetry more generally usable at the cost of abridging the poet's consciousness.

I will say, parenthetically, that I wish the category of expertly made popular poetry had not all but disappeared in this century. In the last century, the best poets did not hesitate to write on occasion simple songs, hymns, or story-poems which were instantly possessed and valued by a larger public. The author of "In Memoriam" also wrote the ballad of "The Revenge." Though societies were formed to unravel the knottier verses of Robert Browning, there are no knots in "The Pied Piper of Hamelin." I think too of James Russell Lowell's "Once to Every Man and Nation," and of Longfellow's "Paul Revere." These are all fine poems, and all of them are perfectly transparent. Perhaps it is their very transparency which has led critics and teachers to fall silent about them, there being no call for learned mediation; and perhaps that silence has helped many of our poets to forget that there is such a thing as a good popular poem.

But now let me take Housman's poem as a miniature specimen of what Mr. Shapiro calls "high art," and defend it against Mr. Shapiro. It is probably not Housman whom Mr. Shapiro is attacking, and yet the strictures might all apply to him. Mr. Shapiro talks as if a poem could be either referential or humanly vital, but not both. Surely you will agree that Housman's poem is both: it is a passionate celebration of courage, prompted one suspects by an immediate occasion; at the same time, and without any dampening of its urgency, it recalls a convention as old as the Greeks, and defends its heroes against detraction through liberal allusions to literature and myth. Mr. Shapiro says that to be referential is to "repeat the past"; Housman most certainly does not do that. What he does is to confront the present with a mind and heart which contain the past. His poem does not knuckle under to a Greek convention, it makes use of that convention and much modifies it. His allusions do not "repeat" Milton and St. Paul, they bring them to bear upon a contemporary event, and in turn they bring that event to bear upon Milton and St. Paul. Milton's good angels are not, in Housman's poem, what they were in *Paradise Lost*; they are transformed by a fresh conjunction; and Housman implicitly quarrels both with the moral exclusiveness of St. Paul and with Milton's idea that righteousness must prevail.

I would uphold Housman's poem as a splendid demonstration of the art of referring. The poem requires a literate reader, but given such a reader it is eminently effective. I selected the poem for discussion precisely because, unlike most of Housman, it is capable of misinterpretation; nevertheless, as I've pointed out, a reader *can* arrive at a just sense of its tone and drift without consciously identifying any of its references. It *all but* delivers its whole meaning right away. One reason why Housman's allusions can be slow in transpiring, as they were for me, is that the words which point toward Milton or St. Paul—such words as "wages" or "earth's foundations"—are perfectly at home in the language of the poem as a whole; and this seems to me a great virtue. In a bad poem, there are often certain words which step out of line, wave their arms, and cry "Follow me! I have overtones!" It takes a master to make references, or what Robert Frost calls "displacements," without in any way falsifying the poem's voice, its way of talking. Now, as for the allusions proper, they are to the Bible, *Paradise Lost,* and Greek mythology, all of which are central to *any* version of our tradition, and in some degree familiar to every educated reader. So familiar are these sources that I'm sure Housman's allusions must unconsciously affect anyone's understanding of the poem, even upon a casual first reading. And I would say that our familiarity with the things to which Housman is referring justifies the subtlety and brevity of his echoes. The poem assumes that the words "wages" and "dead" will suffice to suggest St. Paul, and I think that a fair assumption.

Housman's allusions, once one is aware of them, are not decorative but very hard working. Their chief function is to supplement Housman's explicit praise of the mercenaries with implicit dispraise of their detractors, and so make us certain of the poem's whole attitude toward its subject. To achieve such certainty, however, one need not catch every hint, every echo; any *one* of Housman's references, rightly interpreted, will permit the reader to take confident possession of the poem. I like that. A poem should not be like a double-crostic; it should not be the sort of puzzle in which you get nothing until you get it all. Art doesn't or shouldn't work that way; we are not cheated of a symphony if we fail to react to some passage on the flute, and a good poem should yield itself more than once, offering the reader an early and sure purchase, and deepening repeatedly as he comes to know it better.

This is what happens time and again as one reads and re-reads Housman. In his poem, "On the idle hill of summer," an indolent young man hears the stirring and fatal music of a marching column, and decides to enlist. The final quatrain goes like this:

> Far the calling bugles hollo,
>   High the screaming fife replies,
> Gay the files of scarlet follow:
>   Woman bore me, I will rise.
>     [*A Shropshire Lad,* xxxv]

"Woman bore me, I will rise." He will rise and enlist because "woman bore him"—that is, because he is a man and can't resist the summons of the bugle. The last line is forceful and plain, and clinches the poem beautifully. We need no more. Yet there is more, and perhaps on the second reading, or the fifth, or the twentieth, we may hear in that last line a reverberation of the prayer which is said at the graveside in the Anglican burial service, and which begins: "Man, that is born of a woman, hath but a short time to live, and is full of misery. . . ."

If we do catch that echo, the line gains both in power and in point; but if we don't catch it, we are still possessed of a complete and trustworthy version of Housman's poem. And to speak again of Milton, I think that most of the reverberations in *Paradise Lost* work in the same way. Satan, wakening in the fiery gulf of Hell, says to Beelzebub, who is sprawled at his side:

> If thou beest he; But O how fall'n! how chang'd
> From him, who in the happy Realms of Light
> Cloth'd with transcendent brightness didst outshine
> Myriads though bright . . .

There is a suggestion of Isaiah there which perhaps I might notice unassisted; but I lack the ready knowledge of Virgil which Milton reasonably expected of his reader, and so I am grateful for the scholar's footnote which directs me to Book II of the *Aeneid.* There the shade of Hector appears to Aeneas in a dream, mangled, blackened with dirt, and *quantum mutatus ab illo Hectore* —"how changed" from that Hector who once returned from battle clothed in the bright armor of Achilles! The Virgilian echo is enhancing; it helps to tune the voice of Satan, and the likening of Beelzebub to Hector poignantly stresses the rebel angels' fall from brightness and from heroic strength and virtue. But if there were no footnote to help me, if I never sensed the shade of Hector behind Milton's lines, I should not on that account be balked or misled. I should already have gathered from the surface of the lines one sure and adequate sense of their tone and meaning.

Let me now read you a more dubious example of the art of referring. The poem is by Yeats; it was written in 1909 or 1910, after the poet's reconciliation with Maud Gonne; and its title is "King and No King."

> "Would it were anything but merely voice!"
> The No King cried who after that was King,
> Because he had not heard of anything
> That balanced with a word is more than noise;
> Yet Old Romance being kind, let him prevail
> Somewhere or somehow that I have forgot,
> Though he'd but cannon—Whereas we that had thought
> To have lit upon as clean and sweet a tale
> Have been defeated by that pledge you gave
> In momentary anger long ago;
> And I that have not your faith, how shall I know
> That in the blinding light beyond the grave
> We'll find so good a thing as that we have lost?
> The hourly kindness, the day's common speech,
> The habitual content of each with each
> When neither soul nor body has been crossed.[3]

A great many intelligent readers, including some professional poets of my acquaintance, have found this poem very troublesome. In order to fathom its sixteen lines, one must follow the suggestion of Yeats' title and read *A King and No King*, which is a five-act play by Beaumont and Fletcher first performed in 1611. The play tells how King Arbaces of Iberia conceives an incestuous passion for his sister Panthea, and how his apparently hopeless situation is at last happily resolved by the discovery that Panthea is, after all, *not* his sister. Prior to this fifth-act clarification, Arbaces delivers a number of violent speeches expressing thwarted lust, and one of these Yeats has quoted. Speaking of the words "brother" and "sister," which are the obstacles to his seemingly guilty passion, Arbaces cries, "Let 'em be anything but merely voice"—meaning that if only they were not bodiless words, but concrete things like soldiers or cities, he could turn his cannon on them and destroy them.

Yeats is comparing King Arbaces' frustrated desires to his own, and he is also comparing the words "brother" and "sister," which so vex Arbaces, to some unshakeable pledge or vow made by the lady who is the addressee of his poem. If we look into Richard Ellmann's biography of Yeats, we find that Maud Gonne, in 1909, had informed Yeats "that their relations could be those of a spiritual marriage only," and that she had assured him, "You will not suffer because I will pray." Once we have this information, Yeats' poem becomes perfectly clear: it is a plea for physical as well as spiritual love, and in re-reading it we must put a strong emphasis on the word "body" in the last line.

When one has managed to figure out some puzzling poem, it is natural to be a little foolishly proud; one feels like an insider, an initiate, and one is not inclined to be very critical of a work which has certified one's cleverness and industry. For a few heady weeks in 1954, I thought of myself as the only living understander of Yeats' "King and No King." Since then, however, the number of insiders has grown considerably, and I now feel less proprietary toward the poem, and more objective. There is much to admire in "King and No King": the rhythmic movement is splendidly dramatic; the language slides deftly in and out of the common idiom; in respect of pacing and diction, the poem is a good specimen of that artful recklessness, that *sprezzatura*, which Yeats was aiming at in the first decade of this century. Yet what an inconsistency there is between the blurting, spontaneous manner of the opening lines, and the poet's stubborn withholding of the theme! A good poet knows how, in referring to some little-known thing, to convey without loss of concision some sense of what the reference *must* mean; but Yeats, though he devotes almost seven lines to the Beaumont and Fletcher play, chooses to suppress any suggestion whatever that the play, and his poem, are concerned with frustrated sexual appetite. The consequence is that the reader stumbles badly on the sill of the poem, and never stops staggering until he is out the back door.

There are reasons, I suspect, for Yeats' having used a remote literary reference not only as a source of analogies to his personal predicament, but also as a means of enshrouding his subject matter. The subject is, after all, inherently delicate, and there is also some danger of the ridiculous in an argumentative plea for physical favors, especially if one has known the woman since the late 1880's. But whatever Yeats' reasons for writing as he did—and I have no real business guessing at them—one must wonder about the public value of a poem which mutes its theme by a thoroughly reticent allusion to a little-known text. One must also question the integrity, the artistic self-sufficiency, of any short poem which requires to be grasped through the reading of a bad five-act play and the consultation of a biography.

As the English critic John Press recently said, "There is a popular belief that what conservatives like to call real poetry was perfectly straightforward until some unspecified date, when poets suddenly changed into reckless bunglers or deliberately set out to bamboozle plain, honest readers with mumbo-jumbo." I hope that I don't seem to be offering aid and comfort to the holders of that unhistorical belief. What I do mean to say, in concession to Mr. Shapiro's view of things, is that the art of reference in poetry has become a very difficult art, owing to the incoherence of our culture, and that some poems refer more successfully than others. It is generally agreed, I hope, that one cannot sensibly describe a poem as a direct message from poet to public; but one can say that a poem addresses itself, in I. A. Richards' phrase, to some "condition of the language," and pre-supposes some condition of the culture. Every poem is based on an unformulated impression of what words and things are known and valued in the literate community; every poem is written, as it were, in some intellectual and cultural key. It is therefore possible to say of a poem that, in relation to its appropriate audience, it is tactful or not.

Housman's poem is a model of tact, both in its references and in its manner of referring. Yeats' poem is less tactful, because it cites an ancient play which the most eligible and cultured reader might not know, and which must be known if the poem is to be breached at all. As for the *Cantos* of Ezra Pound, they contain some of the finest passages in modern poetry, but they are supremely tactless. That is, they seem to arise from a despair of any community, and they do not imply a possible audience as Housman's poem does. It is all very well for Pound to claim that his *Cantos* deal "with the usual subjects of conversation between intelligent men"; but intelligent men, though they do talk of history and economics and the arts, do not converse in broken fragments of mythology, unattributed quotations, snatches of Renaissance correspondence, cryptic reminiscences, and bursts of unorthodox Chinese. Pound's presentational manner of writing, which developed out of Imagism, is the method least capable of turning his eccentric erudition into a consistently usable poetry. The advantage of the method is immediacy, and the investment of the idea in the thing, but the method does not work unless the reader knows what it is that is being so immediate. Because the *Cantos* lack any discursive tissue, because they refuse the reader any sort of intercession, even those whose learning exceeds Ezra Pound's cannot be said to be ready for them.

There are three things a reader might do about the *Cantos*. First, he might decide not to read them. Second, he might read them as Dr. Williams recommends, putting up with much bafflement for the sake of the occasional perfect lyric, the consistently clean and musical language, and the masterly achievement of quantitative effects through the strophic balancing of rhythmic masses. Or, thirdly, the reader might decide to understand the *Cantos* by consulting, over a period of years, the many books from which Pound drew his material. At almost every university, nowadays, there is someone who has undertaken that task: he may be identified by the misshapenness of his learning and by his air of lost identity.

None of the three courses I have mentioned is a thoroughly happy one, and the *Cantos* are one proof of Mr. Shapiro's contention that poetry's relations with the past, on the one hand, and with its public on the other, have become problematical. I will grant Mr. Shapiro that there are misuses of the past which can be hurtful to poetry. Antiquarianism is one: the rapt pedantry of Ezra Pound, and the bland, donnish pedantry of certain other poets, alike distract us from the uninterpreted fields and streets and rooms of the present, in which the real battles of imagination must be fought. I will grant, too, that the sense of history can be crippling to poetry if history is so interpreted as to impose some narrow limitation or imperative on the poet. The poet must not feel dwarfed by the literary past, nor should he listen too trustingly to those who say that poetry's role in society is inevitably diminishing. Nor should he adjust his concerns to what others consider the great thought-currents of the times: the *Zeitgeist*, after all, is only a spook invented by the critics. Nor, finally, does poetry prosper when it puts itself wholly at the service of some movement, some institution. I think of Mayakovsky, who wrote "I have subdued myself, setting my heel on the throat of my own song," and who said that he had "cancelled out his soul" the better to serve the socialist age. It may be true, as some say, that Mayakovsky was made by the Revolution; but surely the service of history broke him as well. In all these ways, historical consciousness can paralyze, trivialize or enslave the poet's art; but I am not on that account moved to accept Mr. Shapiro's imperative, which is that poets must now secede from history and dwell in "biological time."

The past which most properly concerns the poet is, as T. S. Eliot has said, both temporal and timeless. It is, above all, a great index of human possibilities. It is a dimension in which we behold, and are beheld by, all those forms of excellence and depravity which men have assumed and may assume again. The poet needs this lively past as a means of viewing the present without provinciality, and of saying much in little; he must hope for the tact and the talent to make that past usable for the audience which his poems imply. My friend John Ciardi once said, "Pompeii is everybody's home town, sooner or later." I should add that for every poet, whatever he may say as critic or polemicist, Pompeii is still a busy quarter of the city of imagination.

# The Nature of Housman's Poetry

## by Christopher Ricks

Housman thought that literary critics were even rarer than poets or saints, so he would not have been surprised that we are hard put to say why we like or dislike his poems. His admirers usually offer little more than pious generalities, and his detractors say "adolescent"—a word used by critics as different as Edmund Wilson, George Orwell, Cyril Connolly, R. P. Blackmur, and Conrad Aiken. There is an excellent annotated bibliography of writings on Housman in *P.M.L.A.* (1945) by R. W. Stallman, who not surprisingly found it necessary to include a section on that famous difficulty, "The Problem of Belief." After speaking of Housman's pessimism, he summarised the critical groupings:

> On the ground of these beliefs his poetry is evaluated thus: (1) The poetry is adversely criticised or rejected on the ground that *his beliefs,* being adolescent, unsound, or without a final standard of value, *interpose obstacles to the enjoyment or appreciation of the poetry;* (2) the poetry is discredited on the ground that *his beliefs,* being agnostic or un-Christian, *are discreditable beliefs;* (3) the poetry, *with his beliefs abstracted,* is valued apart from and in spite of these beliefs; (4) the poetry is valued *because of the beliefs;* the poetry, however pessimistic his beliefs, is "good medicine," an anodyne for the wounds of life.

But there is an odd omission; everyone seems to take it for granted that Housman's poems unwaveringly endorse the pessimistic beliefs which they assert. To me his poems are remarkable for the ways in which rhythm and style temper or mitigate or criticise what in bald paraphrase the poem would be saying. Rhythm and

"The Nature of Housman's Poetry" by Christopher Ricks. From *Essays in Criticism,* XIV (1964), 268–84. Copyright 1964 by Christopher Ricks. Reprinted by permission of the editors of *Essays in Criticism.*

style never abolish the beliefs, and this for the good reason that the beliefs (the urge to pessimism, the need to strike a strong pose) are not abolishable—we can call them adolescent or childish or puerile or immature only if we also concede that there has never been a man adult enough not to feel some magnetic pull from them, some wish to succumb to them, some uncertainty as to whether they are temptations or aspirations.

Housman has often been compared to a child, and not always by those who dislike his poems. A. F. Allison: "It is the attitude of the child whose party has been spoilt" (*R.E.S.*, 1943). Randall Jarrell [see p. 56]: "It has more than a suspicion of the child's *when I'm dead, then they'll be sorry*" (*Kenyon Review*, 1939). His poems often assert positions that are inadequate in ways suggested by calling them adolescent—inadequate not as utterly alien to our experience, or wilfully thought-up, but in the sense that we ought not to be in one mind about them, and should fear that they might be sirens. There are usually three reactions to this "adolescence" of attitude. We may say that what a poem asserts, its attitudes or beliefs, has no bearing on its poetic quality. And here we might call up Housman, who seems at times (but only at times) to be saying this in *The Name and Nature of Poetry*. Or we may say that a poem's beliefs are inseparable from its quality, and that his poems suffer because of the childishness of what they say. Such is the opinion of the most articulate of his detractors. Or we may agree that the beliefs of a poem are inseparable from its quality, but argue that the relationship between belief and the final total meaning may be strange and oblique. This is to argue that in the best of Housman's poems, the childishness of what is said is part of the effect, but only part, and is absorbed to produce something fine and true—though often something that is, quite legitimately, in two minds. Clearly this does not apply to many of his most attractive and simple poems; these I rate less highly not because they are simple but because they are not profound.

A straightforward example. In paraphrase, the poem "I to my perils" says that if you look on the black side you will never be disappointed. Childish, in the narrow sense that it expresses an attitude commoner in children than in adults. Taking an exam at 16, one said "I'm sure I've failed." Childish, too, in the larger

sense, that later on one couldn't but see how little use it actually
was in the face of troubles—indeed, one had a reluctant sense
of that all along. On the other hand, it is also an inextinguishable
attitude; I have not met a man so mature as never to glance wist-
fully towards it as a possible bolt-hole from what is intolerable.
There is no reason why a poem shouldn't express the attitude,
but, yes, there would be something unthinkingly shallow about a
poem which found this advice adequate to the troubles of life. But
if we go from paraphrase (not a rigged one) to the poem itself,
we find something different.

> I to my perils
>   Of cheat and charmer
>   Came clad in armour
>     By stars benign.
> Hope lies to mortals
>   And most believe her,
>   But man's deceiver
>     Was never mine.
>
> The thoughts of others
>   Were light and fleeting,
>   Of lovers' meeting
>     Or luck or fame.
> Mine were of trouble,
>   And mine were steady,
>   So I was ready
>     When trouble came.
>       [*More Poems,* vi]

The poem says a dour glum cramping thing, but how does it say
it? With gaiety and wit that are, if you like, utterly inappropriate.
Instead of the "steady" tramp of military fortitude, there is the
exquisite interlacing of a dance; instead of granite rhymes, there
is a supple effrontery and insouciance that links "charmer" and
"armour," and in so doing surely opposes something to the simple
sturdiness, the indurated hopelessness, of armour. It says that "The
thoughts of others/Were light and fleeting" while "Mine were
of trouble," but whatever the poem may say (in its natural human
wish to find armour for itself, to find steadiness), this cannot be
the case. The movement itself is light and fleeting, and not just

in the lines about others. Just how much difference the movement makes to what in the end is *said,* can be seen when Edmund Wilson [see p. 15], in his excellent essay (*The Triple Thinkers*), quotes these lines but prints them as prose, as a parenthetical gloss on a pessimistic bit of Housman's prose. Housman in this poem may have tried to be a philosopher, but cheerfulness was breaking in. That the poem is not resting smugly in shallow pessimism is borne out by its emphatic closing words: "When trouble came." The Biblical figure who endured all that life could inflict, but who was sustained by something other than a habit of looking on the black side, would have retorted harshly. "Job curseth the day of his birth" (Ch. 3)—a chapter which ends emphatically: "I was not in safety, neither had I rest, neither was I quiet; yet trouble came." If Housman (as Norman Marlow noted) tacitly invokes Job, it is not because he thinks he has found a moral stance which could cope unrepiningly with all that Job suffered, but because he knows he has not. "An ill-favoured thing, sir, but mine own." Housman's position may be inadequate, but it would be ignoble only if he thought it was adequate.

It would not do to claim this as a subtle poem, but it shows the tug of contraries which so often makes for the profoundest of Housman. And it is not adolescent. Louis MacNeice was rebuked in *Scrutiny* (1941) for saying that "Housman uses his tripping measures to express the profoundest pessimism"—"as though," objected Mr. Mellers, "as though the vulgar lilt weren't a comment on the pessimism's profundity." *Vulgar* is never easy to understand; perhaps it is not a useful word in literary criticism. But clearly Mr. Mellers took the lilt as a "comment" on the pessimism only in a derogatory sense. Not in the true sense that the movement of many of Housman's poems comments on, and alters, what they say. We must not support Housman's provocative rearguard action: "Poetry is not the thing said but a way of saying it." Yet the "way" is legitimately part of the total effect, and many of his poems show *what is said* teasingly at odds with *how it is said.* His sense of decorum, in fact, is a larger one than that which oppresses a lot of contemporary verse, where we find that the rhythm and movement simply say again in their own medium what the diction too is saying. A violent expressiveness can become

as tedious as a thrice-told tale; told once by the words themselves,
again by a violence of crowded or jammed rhythms, and a third
time by brutal changes of line-length or stanza-form. As in these
opening lines by a poet of talent, Peter Redgrove:

> Eyes skyward and awash, his gleaming pate
> Moons through the stripping twigs, rinsed
> Sweet and gasping, cracked.
> Blue water gnashing from his eyes
> He struggles up the shrugging of the twigs,
> Rears . . . collapses in his cricks.

It might be objected that Housman left us a clear statement in
*The Name and Nature of Poetry*. He said categorically that "meaning is of the intellect, poetry is not." So how can it be of any use
to explore his meaning? But: (i) critics as unlike as H. W. Garrod
and Cleanth Brooks have agreed that many of Housman's best
effects cannot be encompassed by his theory (as in Wordsworth);
(ii) the theory itself is confused and self-contradictory; (iii) the
contrarieties which underlie many of the best of Housman's poems
are not so much intellectual as emotional, and Housman certainly
did not ask that poetry should be emotionally simple or single-
minded. (Nor are his detailed criticisms of his brother's poems easy
to reconcile with the abdication of intellect in poetry.) Note, for
example, the word "vibration" when he says that the function of
poetry is "to set up in the reader's sense a vibration corresponding
to what was felt by the writer." There "vibration" does not seem
to be simply a loose word for "feeling." Vibration is oscillation,
moving to and fro like a pendulum. Of bad 18th-century verse
he complained that "it could not express human feelings with
a variety and delicacy answering to their own." And his account
of Collins, Cowper, and Blake is not unthinkably far from saying
that the force of their work came from a war within the poems;
these three poets were not altogether mad, "but elements of their
nature were more or less insurgent against the centralised tyranny
of the intellect, and their brains were not thrones on which the
great usurper could sit secure."

Such contrarieties characterise many of his examples in the
lecture. When he wished to commend diction and movement,
why did he choose (good though it is) a stanza by Daniel?

> Come, worthy Greek, Ulysses, come,
> Possess these shores with me:
> The winds and seas are troublesome,
> And here we may be free.
> Here may we sit and view their toil
> That travail in the deep,
> And joy the day in mirth the while,
> And spend the night in sleep.

But the effectiveness of this stanza comes not just from its diction and movement but from a fact unmentioned by Housman: that the Siren speaks to Ulysses. The speaker is disowned or resisted even while we read and are attracted; the movement may be free and mirthful, but the whole sense of the lines is not so, and the movement of Ulysses's reply is significantly harsher. Like the best of Spenser, the emotional effect of Daniel's lines is not simple, and they did not come to Housman's mind just because of their fluent diction and movement.

From "Ode to the Cuckoo," which was either written by John Logan or stolen (why?) by him from Michael Bruce, Housman quoted:

> Sweet bird, thy bower is ever green,
> Thy sky is ever clear;
> Thou hast no sorrow in thy song,
> No winter in thy year.

"A tinge of emotion," said Housman. But once again the effect comes from something implied but not stated, an emotion running counter to the explicitly stated joy which the poem celebrates. The effect of "thy . . . thy . . . thou . . . thy . . . thy" is to set up a keen unspoken sense of what, for others than the migrating cuckoo, is harshly true. There is, as it were, a counterpointed stress: "*Thou* hast no sorrow in *thy* song." The verse may speak of "*no* sorrow" and "*no* winter," but its effect is to leave sorrow and winter undissolved; the mood, on the verge of self-pity, is emotionally various. The stanza is in fact the only good one in a poor poem; but if we put it back in context we find that implicit in it (and finely so) is all that the surrounding stanzas so miserably spell out:

What time the pea puts on the bloom
    Thou fliest thy vocal vale,
An annual guest in other lands,
    Another Spring to hail.

Sweet bird! thy bower is ever green,
    Thy sky is ever clear;
Thou hast no sorrow in thy song,
    No winter in thy year!

O could I fly, I'd fly with thee!
    We'd make, with joyful wing,
Our annual visit o'er the globe,
    Companions of the Spring.

All those unattainable aspirations so poorly spelled out in "O could I fly, I'd fly with thee," all the chafing at the fact that even in speaking of the cuckoo's joy one could not but invoke sorrow— all these were contained in the stanza Housman quoted. He liked it, not because it was "tinged with emotion," but because it was tinged with conflicting emotions.

The same is true of Housman's highest example, once again a phrasing which is touchingly simple and yet assaulted by feelings which deny it:

Duncan is in his grave;
After life's fitful fever he sleeps well.

These lines would hardly be the same if they were spoken by a pious old man reconciled to death, and not by Macbeth, guiltily jealous of Duncan still, even now; guiltily exonerating himself too (Duncan is now better off); on the verge of self-pity, fitful and feverous and yet creating a momentary and precarious peace in thinking of a death which nevertheless he will defy to the utmost. The lines are an oasis in Macbeth's speech—but a delusion or a sudden understanding?

But let the frame of things disjoint, both the worlds suffer,
Ere we will eat our meal in fear, and sleep
In the affliction of these terrible dreams,
That shake us nightly. Better be with the dead,
Whom we, to gain our peace, have sent to peace,

> Than on the torture of the mind to lie
> In restless ecstasy. Duncan is in his grave;
> After life's fitful fever he sleeps well;
> Treason has done his worst; nor steel, nor poison,
> Malice domestic, foreign levy, nothing
> Can touch him further!                    (III, ii. 16–26)

"*He* sleeps well"; it is hardly right to return to "Thou hast no sorrow in *thy* song," but here too it will have been the swelling of self-pity that drew Housman's attention. That, and the conflict lying behind the simple lines, a conflict made hideously explicit when Macbeth speaks of gaining peace, and when he utters words that are, literally speaking, nonsensical: when he says that the world may fall *before* he will suffer that which he *already* suffers, "these terrible dreams."

In defending his position, Housman was willing to say that Shakespeare sometimes wrote nonsense. But once again his example is of a certain kind of emotional undercurrent:

> Even Shakespeare, who had so much to say, would sometimes pour out his loveliest poetry in saying nothing.

> > Take O take those lips away
> > > That so sweetly were forsworn,
> > And those eyes, the break of day,
> > > Lights that do mislead the morn;
> > But my kisses bring again,
> > > > bring again,
> > Seals of love, but seal'd in vain,
> > > > seal'd in vain.

> That is nonsense; but it is ravishing poetry.

Housman does not say that the lines are meaningless; nonsense is a different thing. And in one important way this song is nonsense; how can you bring kisses back again? The force of the song surely comes from the fact that the powerful undertow of its feeling is so much at odds with what it is asserting (much as the force of Tennyson's "Ulysses" comes from the contrast between the robust sentiments and the slow-wheeling verse). The song may say that the false lover must "Take O take those lips away," but somehow it doesn't turn out like that; the sorrowing

repetitions show us an attachment that is still very much alive, refusing to accept that the false lover is false and ought to send back
the kisses much as a gentleman sends back old love-letters. And the
context of the song (*Measure for Measure,* Act IV) brings out very
clearly these double feelings. It is sung at Mariana's instigation;
she still loves Angelo although he falsely broke his promise to her.
The song *purports* to be addressed to a woman; part of its force
comes from this transference, a wishful turning of the tables which
makes the woman the powerful one who is pleaded with. The
Duke had said to Isabella in Act III: "This fore-named maid hath
yet in her the continuance of her first affection: his unjust unkindness (that in all reason should have quenched her love) hath (like
an impediment in the current) made it more violent and unruly."
Altogether apt to Housman, whose poems again and again show
the continuance of emotions which should in all reason have been
quenched, so that it is the impediment itself which results in the
force of feeling. We never hear all of Mariana's song (many of
Housman's best poems are fragments), because the Duke enters,
disguised as a friar, and Mariana dismisses the boy who has sung
it:

> Break off thy song, and haste thee quick away,
> Here comes a man of comfort, whose advice
> Hath often still'd my brawling discontent.
> I cry you mercy, Sir, and well could wish
> You had not found me here so musical.
> Let me excuse me, and believe me so,
> My mirth it much displeas'd, but pleas'd my woe.
>
> *Duke:* 'Tis good; though music oft hath such a charm
> To make bad, good; and good provoke to harm.

It was just this power that drew Housman, the power of music
radically to change what is said. To make bad good, and "nonsense"
sense? The sequence of Mariana's words suggests that she will no
longer need the song *because* "Here comes a man of comfort . . .";
and when she speaks of "*brawling* discontent" we return to the
stream unruly because of impediments. She has to apologise for
the song, and the Duke does not accept the simple plea that it will
have made her feel appropriately sad. The "charm" of the song

is as much magic as delight; will it bring Angelo back even while it urges him (her) to go? "His unjust unkindness (that in all reason should have quenched her love)"—what the song presents is the co-existence of that love with a keen sense of that unkindness, and yet with the sexes reversed. The combination touched Housman.

It was a tug of this kind, against the explicit meaning, of which Housman spoke in the most famous passage of his lecture:

> In these six simple words of Milton—
>
> Nymphs and shepherds, dance no more—
>
> what is it that can draw tears, as I know it can, to the eyes of more readers than one? What in the world is there to cry about? Why have the mere words the physical effect of pathos when the sense of the passage is blithe and gay? I can only say, because they are poetry, and find their way to something in man which is obscure and latent. . . .

Housman is well aware that there is nothing to cry about, and that the sense is blithe and gay. He simply says that there is also a strong counterfeeling of sadness. F. W. Bateson attacked vigorously:

> The pathos of Milton's six simple words obviously derives for Housman from the last two of them. As Shenstone had pointed out in the middle of the eighteenth century, "the words 'no more' have a singular pathos; reminding us at once of past pleasure, and the future exclusion of it." But Milton's injunction to the nymphs and shepherds was not, in fact, to stop dancing, but to "dance no more/By sandy *Ladons* Lillied banks." The nymphs were only to transfer their dances from Arcadia to Harefield in Middlesex. . . . Housman's tears came from taking Milton's line out of its context and giving it a meaning it was never intended to have. By misreading Milton he has created what is essentially his own private poem. (*English Poetry,* 1950, pp. 15–16.)

Housman's "own private poem," not surprisingly, resembles his own poems. But somehow the Shenstone passage seems slightly to support Housman, and one thinks of Tennyson's "So sad, so fresh the days that are no more" or of his early poem "O sad

*No more!* O sweet *No more!"* In the song from *Arcades,* Milton does
after all leave us with that momentary hesitation (at least on the
brink of pathos) which comes from having the line end at "no
more"—there is a feeling that the line *could* be sad though de-
lightfully it turns out not to be. Certainly the main sense is gay,
but is there something of an undertow, just as there is in the
*Nativity Ode* when "The Nimphs in twilight shade of tangled
thickets mourn"? It is interesting that "twilight" (with its associations of sad beauty) is found too in the song, in conjunction with
nymphs; indeed the song concedes that to move one's home even
on such a noble occasion cannot be achieved without some sadness
to someone (one reason why it is a great compliment to the
Countess of Derby):

> Nymphs and Shepherds dance no more
>     By sandy *Ladons* Lillied banks.
> On old *Lycæus* or *Cyllene* hoar,
>     Trip no more in twilight ranks,
> Though *Erymanth* your loss deplore,
>     A better soyl shall give ye thanks . . .

Housman was certainly over-sensitive to the pathos, and he leaves
the impression that it obliterates the explicit joy of the lines. But
some pathos there is ("Though *Erymanth* your loss deplore"). Once
again one of his examples is characterised by conflicting emotions,
as on this occasion he expressly noted: "Why have the mere words
the physical effect of pathos when the sense of the passage is blithe
and gay?"

Housman took provocativeness to the point of silliness when
he called the song from *Measure for Measure* "nonsense," but
this would be less absurd if we connected it with "nonsense-verse."
Nonsense-verse is not meaningless, and the sense of it matters; its
emotional force comes from the disparity between the absurdity or
falsity of what is said and the emotional truth of what is felt. The
childishness or cruelty is combined with a jauntiness, wit, and
aplomb of style and movement. John Wain, speaking of the great
difficulty which many 19th-century poets had in breaking free of
responsibilities and saying what was in their minds, strikingly
juxtaposed Hopkins and the nonsense-poets. He quoted Edward
Lear:

> There was an old man who screamed out
> Whenever they knocked him about . . .

"A modern writer might well begin a poem in this way, but he
would not pretend that he was doing it to amuse the children"
(British Academy Lecture, 1959). Housman wrote a good deal
of nonsense verse; Laurence Housman included 12 examples in
*A.E.H.*, and 3 more were separately reprinted. H. W. Garrod took
the view that "the nonsense verse was well worth having—who had
believed, else, that Housman had it in him either to be happy or
to write nonsense?" But were Carroll and Lear happy? And much
of Housman's serious verse uses a method—of indirections, disparities, and emotional cross-currents—that is at its clearest in
nonsense-verse. What is said is not what is meant, but something
is certainly meant. (Often one cannot but think that a Freudian
thing is meant.) When you met an old man "whose nerves had
given way," you "attended to his wants": by putting his head into
the ants' nest, tying his hands, and filling his mouth with hay:

> He could not squeal distinctly,
>     And his arms would not go round;
> Yet he did not leave off making
>     A discontented sound.

What more natural at this than mild irritation?

> And I said "When old men's nerves give way,
>     How hard they are to please!"

Such a poem is not an allegory, but how long is it since madness
was treated in such a way? And how and why was Wilde punished?
"Oh they're taking him to prison for the colour of his hair"—
that poem is in a way the greatest of Housman's nonsense-verses,
moving out into a larger lunacy. "The Crocodile, *or* Public Decency" shows us how children, made ashamed of nakedness, sacrifice
themselves when the crocodile calls:

> "Come, awful infant, come and be
> Dressed, if in nothing else in me."

Such poems—and there are many more—are not lacking in personal
feelings; their force comes from the fact that no man could have

had a more rigid sense of Public Decency than had Housman, even though in one vital respect it oppressed his deepest feelings.

Both the nonsense-verse, then, and *The Name and Nature of Poetry* offer evidence that contrarieties and disparities of feeling fascinated Housman. In many of his more strangely powerful poems, the force comes from what is submerged, "obscure and latent," so it is not surprising that he was fond of that particular kind of pun which creates its double meaning by invoking but excluding. When Milton described something in Paradise as "wanton," his meaning did not just forget about the fallen sense of the word; it invoked it but excluded it, so that Eve's hair was "wanton (not *wanton*)." As the man waited to be hanged in Housman's "Eight O'Clock," he "heard the steeple/Sprinkle the quarters on the morning town." Morning (not mourning)": the town does not mourn.

> The diamond tears adorning
> Thy low mound on the lea,
> Those are the tears of morning,
> That weeps, but not for thee.
> [*Last Poems*, xxvii]

"Morning (not mourning)." George Herbert, in "The Sonne," had applauded the English language:

> How neatly doe we give one onely name
> To parents issue and the sunnes bright starre!

Housman, more lugubriously but no more absurdly, relished the conflict between morning and mourning. When the nettle dances on the grave, "It nods and curtseys and recovers." "Recovers," as a term in dancing; the dead man does not recover in this or any (unspoken) sense. "Curtseys," as part of the dance; but the curtsey is hardly a courtesy—indeed to dance on a grave is traditionally the extreme discourtesy.

Housman's sure feeling for a subterranean link comes out in the finest such unspoken pun, in the magnificent and solitary reflection:

> When the bells justle in the tower
> The hollow night amid,

> Then on my tongue the taste is sour
> Of all I ever did.
>
> [*Additional Poems,* ix]

When Laurence Housman printed this, he gave the alternative reading "Then to my heart the thought is sour." Without "tongue" and "taste," almost nothing is left. And this is not just because an immediacy of detail is lost. The almost uncanny connection between the sound of bells and the sour taste depends on "tongue." Bells have tongues. Emily Dickinson, a poet greater than Housman but not utterly different in kind, begins a poem:

> It was not Death, for I stood up,
> And all the Dead, lie down—
> It was not Night, for all the Bells
> Put out their Tongues, for Noon.

Housman was not punning; he would have been perfectly happy if the obscure force of his stanza (which he never published, though it seems to me one of the finest things he ever wrote) had come home without any sense of the bizarre, almost surrealist, connection between the bells and the taste. "Surrealist" may go too far, but it is worth remembering that the first (unauthorised) printing of these lines (1930) bore the title: "A Fragment preserved by oral tradition and said to have been composed by A. E. Housman in a dream." And what is the sourest taste of all?

> Instead of sweets, his ample palate took
> Savour of poisonous brass and metal sick.
> (Keats, *Hyperion,* I. 188–9.)

What is still easily the best discussion of Housman, that by Randall Jarrell [see p. 51] in the *Kenyon Review* (1939), brings out clearly and wittily the antagonisms in two poems: "Crossing alone the nighted ferry," with its love sliding over into contempt and self-contempt, so that it is almost as if there were two poems occupying the same space; and "It nods and curtseys and recovers," where the beautiful syntactical ambiguity of *of* (as in the murderstory *Murder of My Aunt,* where it turns out that the aunt does the murdering) suggests that if a man kills himself for love, it

is too for love of the grave: "The lover of the grave, the lover/That
hanged himself for love." Mr. Jarrell deals deftly with those who
would murmur "adolescent":

> Nor is this a silly adolescent pessimism peculiar to Housman, as so
> many critics assure you. It is better to be dead than alive, best of all
> never to have been born—said a poet approvingly advertised as
> seeing life steadily and seeing it whole. . . . The attitude is obviously
> inadequate and just as obviously important.

But certainly a full-scale defence of Housman would have to
reply in detail to the important charges of "failure of specification"
and of "violence to common experience" that were brought by
John Crowe Ransom (*Southern Review*, 1940) and by F. R. Leavis
(*Scrutiny*, 1945). Mr. Ransom attacked "With rue my heart is
laden," partly on the grounds that one of its images "runs counter
to the ironic intention"—but elsewhere Housman made good use
of such running counter. And Dr. Leavis's extremely forceful remarks on "Wake: the silver dusk returning" depend on our being
quite certain that Housman has simply blundered into "insensitive
falsity" and is not *using* it.

My final example is one of Housman's best poems. Yet it does
apparently take up an attitude that is almost silly or absurd. In
"Tell me not here, it needs not saying," William Empson noticed
the way in which each penultimate line breaks into Alcaics, and
then offered a superb insight into how the poem works:

> I think the poem is wonderfully beautiful. But a secret gimmick
> may well be needed in it to overcome our resistances, because the
> thought must be about the silliest or most self-centered that has
> ever been expressed about Nature. Housman is offended with the
> scenery, when he pays a visit to his native place, because it does not
> remember the great man; this is very rude of it. But he has described
> it as a lover, so in a way the poem is only consistent to become jealous
> at the end. Perhaps the sentiment has more truth than one might
> think . . . many English painters really are in love with the scenery
> of England, and nothing else, so they had much better give up their
> theoretical tiff with Nature and get back to painting it. The last
> verse of the poem, driving home the moral, is no longer tenderly
> hesitant and therefore has given up the Alcaic metre.
>
> (*British Journal of Aesthetics*, 1962)

Housman's attitude, which would be little more than silly if concerned only with Nature, turns into a curious kind of jealousy if it deals too with love of a woman. Of course the poem is magnificent as natural description; Housman's eye and ear were never more alert. But this straightforward, respectable and explicit feeling is entwined with a remarkable erotic force. Not that the poem is "really" erotic and not about Nature; it is about both. Housman, with disconcerting literalness, really does write about his mistress Nature as if she were his mistress. Hence the peculiar force derived from casting the poem in the form of a monologue from an old and cast-off lover to the young man who has succeeded him. You need not tell *me* about her, "for she and I were long acquainted." So that the act of resigning (a resignation stated, but still showing "the continuance of [his] first affection") is fraught with an intensity hard to understand if we think only of Nature:

> Possess, as I possessed a season,
> The countries I resign.

Housman is taking seriously two conventions that are usually trifled with: that Nature is like a mistress, and that loving a mistress is like loving Nature (the long vogue for poems which describe love-making in topographical terms). There is the contrast between the unhurried rhythm and the momentary flash of bitterness in "a season," and there is the complete aptness of "Possess," emphatically placed and repeated. The enchantress was not just distantly *heard* on the new-mown grass or under the trees.

> On acres of the seeded grasses
> The changing burnish heaves . . .

Are we to remember how Tennyson brings together love and Nature in *Locksley Hall?*

> In the Spring a livelier iris changes on the burnish'd dove;
> In the Spring a young man's fancy lightly turns to thoughts
> of love.

And surely it is not just of Nature as *like* a mistress that we think when we hear how

full of shade the pillared forest
Would murmur and be mine.

The poem is not a code, and we cannot go through it looking for
point-by-point correspondences. What we have is the co-existence
of powerful love for Nature with powerful erotic feelings. It is in
the last stanza that the bitterness makes itself heard; the poet is
still in love with something he knows is heartless and witless (no
substitute for the love of people). Lurking behind this attack
on the faithless promiscuity of Nature is the traditional image
for a promiscuous woman as "the wide world's common place,"
or "the bay where all men ride." Bitterness, perversity, and self-
reproach are all fused by lyrical grace into a poem unique in the
language. "What tune the enchantress plays"—no wonder Housman remembered that stanza from Daniel's "Ulysses and the Siren":

Come, worthy Greek, Ulysses, come,
Possess these shores with me . . .

As the Duke said in *Measure for Measure*, "music oft hath such
a charm/To make bad, good; and good provoke to harm."

# The Whole of Housman

## by Morton Dauwen Zabel

In 1894 A. E. Housman, having been given a manuscript of his brother's poems to read, sent that prolific author a minutely detailed criticism that included the following sentences:

> What makes many of your poems more obscure than they need be is that you do not put yourself in the reader's place and consider how, and at what stage, that man of sorrows is to find out what it is all about. You are behind the scenes and know all the data; but he knows only what you tell him. It appears . . . that in writing that precious croon you had in your head some meaning of which you did not suffer to escape one drop into what you wrote: you treat us as Nebuchadnezzar did the Chaldeans, and expect us to find out the dream as well as the interpretation.

The irony here requires no italics. Two years later Housman published the book that sped his fame through the English-speaking world. *A Shropshire Lad* caught the pathos of its generation; its accents of loss and regret are fixed in the consciousness of all modern readers, and its croon has been judged sufficiently precious; but the grimly disciplined poignance that forms its claim and appeal to the world, though sometimes quavering toward intimacy or revelation, remained to the end of Housman's life masked and inscrutable.

That inscrutability was the mark and habit of his character. By the age of thirty-seven he had set his back implacably on the vivacity of spirit that had once made him the gayest member of his family. He had weathered the crushing blow of failure in

Greats at Oxford; he had fallen under the "heavy change" that made him a stranger to his relatives. Ten years of drudging service in the Patent Office had passed like a slow purgatory, varied only by solitary labor under the gas lamps of the British Museum, where he won the mastery of classical texts that was rewarded in 1892 by the Latin professorship at the University of London. Long before he reached the middle of his road, Housman had withdrawn into the secret fastness of his nature. Robinson alone among modern poets offers a comparable figure of mute austerity; Conrad's abrupt check to intimacy or confidence in his personal writings becomes almost genial by contrast. "Can you get him to talk? I can't!" cried Robert Bridges on one occasion; and when Housman was told that Wilfrid Blunt, speaking in his diaries of a visit from the poet, had said, "He would, I think, be quite silent if he were allowed to be," he answered, "That is absolutely true."

Silence is the initial condition of Housman's poetry, as it was the token of a painful diminution of personality that befell him at the outset of adult life. His verse was set from the beginning, by an almost violent mandate, in a fixed and deliberate mold. It offers no characteristic modern pattern of growth, experiment, and discovery. Only Hardy's shows as undeviating an identity from first to last. His distance from the great poets of tragedy or pessimism— agonized, rebellious, impressionable—is great: not only from Baudelaire, Verlaine, and Villon, for whom he expressed a distaste, or from Heine, whose continuous influence brought so little of the German's critical wit and exhilaration into his lyrics, or from Arnold and Hardy, whom he admired above all his contemporaries, but from Pascal and Leopardi, those two stricken witnesses of the dark abyss and the frightening heavens, whom he "studied with admiration" and whose anguished vision and starlit shudders are sometimes caught in his own finest songs. Beyond any of these brothers in darkness he stifled his agony before the mystery and fatality of life. His lyrics speak from the threshold of silence itself. Had their discipline become as absolute as the one he imposed on his practical emotions, his poems would have receded wholly into the reserve that marked Housman's outward character.

That discipline was as final as any poet, short of the defeat of his gifts, could make it. Housman's first problem as a lyrist was to perfect a form and language exactly expressive of the extreme mandate of will he imposed on his sensibility. He once admitted Heine, Shakespeare's songs, and the Border ballads as his models but was "surprised" at the imputation of Latin and Greek influences. But these cannot be slighted. Housman's whole temper, recognizing its suspension between an active poetic impulse and a willed surrender of it, between an instinctive fervor for life and a tragic denial of its value, sharpens toward irony, seeks resolution in the ambiguity of epigram, and tends to express the ingrowth of its forces and the tension of its faculties in a salient virtue of the Latin lyric style—its integrity of structure, its verbal and tonal unity, its delicate stasis of form. What it gave him—as did the Elizabethans, among whom he once called Jonson his master— were the interlocking balances and inversions of phrase, the distributed reference in nouns and pronouns, the hovering ambiguity of particles, the reflexive dependence of verbs and subjects that give his stanzas their tightness and pith. Had he coerced a purely modern and explicit English into these structures he would have produced a language continuously—instead of intermittently— stilted. But here one of his strongest sympathies came to his rescue —his love of folk speech. The aphoristic tang and irony of peasant idiom, grafted to the sophistication of the Horatian style, relaxed his temper, freed it from formulated stiffness and cliché, and gave Housman his true and single medium as a poet—a verse style marked by a subtle irony of tragic suggestion, a tensile integrity of phrasing, a sense of haunting human appeals playing against the grim inexorability of law. In that medium, rising above the inertness of a formula and the desperate repression of his impulses, he wrote his finest poems.

These, now that his work stands complete, no longer appear in some of his most quoted lyrics, those that cast his thought into the inflexibly didactic form that is always the bane of a negative temperament. The lesser Housman, the one most vulnerable to parody, imitation, and personal attack, is seen wherever his lyric style hardens into such inflexibility and his pessimism into the hortatory despair that becomes by inversion sentimental. Originally, it appears, Housman had an extremely uncertain taste in words and meters. He was fond of the singsong lilt or chant used in rather tawdry and superficial poems like "Atys," "The Land of Biscay," and "Far known to sea and shore." Of "Atys" ("Lydians, lords of Hermus river, Sifters of the golden loam") he once said that he was so fond of the rhythm that he always doubted the merit of any poem in which he succumbed to its attraction. He came to guard himself from that music as he guarded his emotional impulses from the appeals of common life and friendship. At both ends of his narrow lyric range, as at both ends of his emotional character, he exercised a ruthless vigilance: here from the spontaneity of feelings that had to be canceled, there from the violence of a censorship so strong that it could end not merely in silence but in emotional paralysis and the logic of suicide. Recoiling from instinctive music or feeling, he produced poems of an opposite extreme: of a deadly and inverted romanticism, of a pessimism so imperative and bare of realistic qualities that they produce a repellent travesty of his talent. Here the Latinized concentration bristles with guards to emotion, and starkness of vision becomes as cloying as the lines in which he rings changes on the ale, the lads, the night, the noose, and the gallows to the point of comic surfeit. It appears at its worst in "Think no more, lad," "The Welsh Marches," "Say, lad, have you things to do," "Others, I am not the first," "The laws of God," "Yonder see the morning blink," "The Immortal Part," and "The Culprit." The authentic part of his talent demanded escape from confines as laming as these, and it is only when he gives some voice to the instinctive delight of his senses, to memories of lost youth, or to responses to nature, that he arrives at the finer sincerity of "With rue my heart," "On Wenlock Edge," "Far in a western brookland," and "The Merry Guide." He succeeds best of all when the repressed emotion becomes externalized, released from an iron-clad vigilance, adopts a dramatic mask or situation, and so takes on the life and pathos of genuine lyric realism: when, in "Bredon Hill," "Hughley Steeple," "Is my team ploughing," "To an Athlete," "I to my perils," "In valleys green and still," and "With seed the sowers scatter," he resolves the hostilities of his nature to their finest delicacy and harmony, avoids both the curt asperity and the occasional Aeschylean pomp of which he was capable, and contributes exquisite poems to the English lyric tradition.

They succeed, moreover, in revealing and relaxing the enigmatic nature of the man who wrote them and in dissolving the contradiction that gave him his quality as a character. They make credible the tyrant of Latin texts who could flay rivals or sycophants alive, yet who led a life of painful loneliness and who, given evidences of affection, described their effect as "almost overwhelming"; the solitary who called himself a Cyrenaic but who favored Epicureans above Stoics; the critic who disliked democracy and defended slavery but who protested the tyranny of the laws of God and man and pleaded for the felon taken to prison "for the color of his hair"; the man who enjoyed bitterness and kept notebooks carefully indexing his vituperations but who saw himself in T. E. Lawrence's words as stricken by "a craving to be liked— so strong and nervous that . . . the terror of failure in an effort so important made me shrink from trying"; the recluse who was contemptuous of comfort and flattery but who told a young American admirer, "Certainly I have never regretted the publication of my poems. The reputation which they brought me, though it gives me no lively pleasure, is something like a mattress interposed between me and the hard ground."

He was complex obviously and an eccentric certainly, a personality of laming deficiencies and self-persecuting logic; a lyric artist of the most limited order. He lends himself almost naively to J. Bronowski's attack (in *The Poet's Defence*) as a victim of inverted sentiment from whose "welter of standards" little emerges but a cancelation of feelings almost antiphonal in regularity and as a self-belittler who took evasive refuge in negations of life, of emotion, of the nature and meaning of poetry itself. Housman's admirers have done him the disservice of blind adulation; his detractors, with the added cooperation of his own perverseness and inconsistency of temperament, will go to inevitable extremes. There are even severer measures of his stature. The cry of despair has sounded in modern poetry, as in ancient, with an anguish but also with an illumination that Housman seldom or never attains. *"Wer wenn ich schriee, hörte mich denn aus der Engel Ordnungen?"* [Who, if I cried out, would hear me then from among the orders of angels? (Rilke, *Duino Elegies*)]. "Selfwrung, selfstrung, sheathe- and shelterless, thoughts against thoughts in groans grind." "I must lie down where all the ladders start/In the foul rag-and-bone shop of my heart." *"L'Irréparable ronge avec sa dent maudite/Notre Dâme."* Of the protest, intensity, and courage of these castings down of spirit he dared little, and his loss in range and force of character is inevitable.

Yet as we now see Housman in his full stature, as the obscurity of his temperament begins to wane, so also the exacerbation of his emotion and his evasion of responsible feeling begin to take on the alleviation of what at its best becomes a subtle and ennobling lyric dignity, a mastery of selfhood and of style that surmounts the imposed denials of his life and the implacable tragedy he saw there but, having seen and faced it, refused to disguise from himself. What that tragedy was is too much a part of the complex of his nature and his poems to bear crude expression, but this much he makes unmistakable: it was his realization that he was destined to live a life deprived of human love. That fact, implicit everywhere, is written clearly enough into the poems on pages 28, 66, 68, 114, 187, 221, and 233.[1] Whatever irresolution exists in his book is a reflection of the contradiction imposed on his faculties by nature itself; the pervading frustration resulted from an intelligence that permitted no blinkers before the fact. But concealed in Housman's nature, masked by his forbidding exterior and his scholarly isolation, existed the true stuff of the poet, once free and impulsive but surviving even its later curtailment, and he was strong enough to make of that conflict the strength and charm of his poems. The science and realism that permit us to see the errors or defects of men also impose the responsibility of understanding them. Outside his poems Housman made that understanding difficult enough, and even inside his verse the slightest comparision with Baudelaire and Hopkins, Yeats and Rilke, immediately gives the measure of his lower station. Yet if he ate of the shadow so long that he became something of the shadow of a man, he at least refused to lapse into sullen silence over the whole wretched business of existence. His endurance was the sign of his character, and the lyrics he wrested from grief and discipline are the mark of his true, if minor, genius. He is one of the most complete instances in literature of the man

[1] *A Shropshire Lad,* xv, xliv, xlv; *Last Poems,* xiv; *More Poems,* xxviii; *Additional Poems,* vi, xviii.

determined to live by will alone, and his lyrics too often reveal what the discipline of will does to a poet. Yet the discipline was real, and its reward came when his suppressed forces broke from him in the form of an exact and exquisite art. It saved him from languor and annihilation, and in the complete book of his songs, standing between the perils of sense and insistence of death, are the lyrics that hold their permanent beauty. They sufficiently redeem his title as a poet and bring to mind what his friend A. C. Benson once said in assaying the talent of Edward FitzGerald, a fellow-sharer with Housman of the melancholy shadows of life:

> The process of estimating the character even of the best of men must be of the nature of addition and subtraction. It is the final total that is our main concern. . . . There can be little question on which side the balance lies. We may regret the want of strenuousness, the overdeveloped sensibility, which led him to live constantly in the pathos of the past, the pain of the contemplation of perishable sweetness. But we may be thankful . . . that the long, quiet years were not misspent which produced, if so rarely, delicate flowers of genius. To enrich the world with one imperishable poem, to make music of some of the saddest and darkest doubts that haunt the mind of man—this is what many far busier and more concentrated lives fail to do. . . . To touch despair with beauty—this is to bear a part in the work of consoling men, of reconciling fate, of enlightening doom, of interpreting the vast and awful mind of God. Truth itself can do no more than hint at the larger hope.

# The Poetry of Emphasis

## by F. W. Bateson

### I

The author of *Poems by Terence Hearsay*—a collection now better known as *A Shropshire Lad*, the title suggested by Housman's friend A. W. Pollard of the British Museum—was also the Professor of Latin at University College, London. By the time *Last Poems* came out in 1922 he was the Kennedy Professor of Latin at Cambridge and a Fellow of Trinity College in that university: a man, in short, at the top of the academic tree. It is natural, therefore, for the critic of Housman's poetry to ask what connection there is, if indeed there is any at all, between the pseudo-Salopian Terence, who put down "Pints and quarts of Ludlow beer" and whose best friend murdered another farm labourer called Maurice (*A Shropshire Lad,* viii)—and the acidulous scholar who freely admitted that he had never actually spent much time in Shropshire. The question is more insistent in Housman's case than in that of such other scholar-poets as Milton or Gray, partly because of the wider gap between the particular poetic persona he adopted and the man himself, and partly because of the element of autobiography, usually veiled though often unconcealed, that is present in his best poems.

An aspect of the Housman problem to which I shall be returning later in this essay is that he was a homosexual. The lines beginning "Oh who is that young sinner with the handcuffs on his wrists?" (first published after Housman's death in Laurence Housman's memoir of his brother) can have no other meaning. Another post-

humous poem (*More Poems*, xxxi) that seems to be even more
directly autobiographical begins:

> Because I liked you better
> Than suits a man to say,
> It irked you, and I promised
> To throw the thought away.

But a critic's first concern is with the poems as poems and not
with the neuroses of his poet. At least twenty of Housman's poems
are likely to live as long as the language. If these poems continue to
tease and fascinate the critical reader today, as I think they do, he
will want to define to himself the special *literary* quality that they
have. It is a quality almost unprecedented in English poetry that
can, I think, be shown to derive from Housman's exceptional
sensitivity to both English and Latin considered simply as languages. Looking round for some clue to connect Terence Hearsay
with the Cambridge Latinist (whose *magnum opus* was a definitive
edition of the almost unreadable *Astronomica* of Manilius), I
remembered a book that my own classical tutor had made me
read when I was a schoolboy. The book is Sidney T. Irwin's once
famous *Clifton School Addresses*, which has a characteristically sug-
gestive dictum in a lecture with the title "Why We Learn Latin."
Why should the writer who aspires to write good English also learn
Latin? "We learn Latin," Irwin answers, "because the merits of this
language are not the merits of ours, and its defects not our defects."
If this is indeed true, it may help to explain the peculiar flavour
of Housman's poetry. The bitter, cynical-sentimental tone of
voice is no doubt that of a homosexual rejected both by his
friend and by society, but bitterness *per se* is not a recipe for a
good poem. As Mallarmé is said to have reminded Degas (who
had good ideas but somehow could not make a poem out of them),
"Poetry is made out of words." (*The best words in the best order.*)
It would be absurd, of course, to suggest that Housman became
the foremost Latinist of his generation simply in order to improve
his English. What can be said, however, is that his expertness in
the Latin language left an indelible imprint on both his English
prose style and his poetry. A fact that is often overlooked is that
he had proved in a series of articles in the specialist journals

his mastery of Latin poetry—and to a lesser extent of Greek poetry too—*before* he had written any of the English poems for which he is remembered, or almost any English poems at all. Of the 105 poems in the two collections that he published himself not one is known to have been written before 1890, though "1887" (*A Shropshire Lad*, i), which is about Queen Victoria's Golden Jubilee, was presumably written in that year. But most of the poems in *A Shropshire Lad* date from 1895, when Housman was already a mature scholar with an international reputation. Any occasional adolescence in these poems is in the subject-matter and not in the treatment or style. "I did not begin to write poetry in earnest," Housman explained to a young French admirer towards the end of his life, "until the really emotional part of my life was over." [1]

The poetry that was written in earnest was written by the Professor of Latin and most of it in Housman's thirty-sixth or thirty-seventh year. For the rest of his life he continued, more intermittently, to write what are essentially the same poems. Some further implications of this late discovery of himself as a poet are worth underlining. One is that the author of *A Shropshire Lad* was already a virtuoso in English prose. By 1895, in articles, lectures, and reviews, Housman had shown himself a master of that pungent contempt for lesser minds which culminated in the fine art of disrespect later displayed in the prefaces to his editions of Manilius, Juvenal, and Lucan.

The Housman of 1895, then, knew exactly what he was doing. When *A Shropshire Lad* was rejected by the publishing establishment, from Macmillan's downward, and Housman had to pay for the book's publication out of his own pocket, he even made a poem (*A Shropshire Lad*, lxiii) out of his own discomfiture:

> I hoed and trenched and weeded,
> And took the flowers to fair:
> I brought them home unheeded;
> The hue was not the wear.

This is not the voice of a poet who has failed. He *knew* that he was writing unfashionable poetry, but he also knew with a self-confi-

---

[1] The letter is dated February 5, 1933, and was addressed to Maurice Pollet, who published it in *Études anglaises*, September, 1937.

dence similar to Horace's *Exegi monumentum aere perennius* that
for Housman too

> here and there will flower
> The solitary stars.

Although it may not be immediately clear to the modern reader,
*A Shropshire Lad* bears much the same disrespectful relation to
the poetry of its period that his devastating review of Schulze's
*Catullus* (*Classical Review*, viii, 1894), for example, bears to its
scholarship. This was the "decadent" phase of English Romanti-
cism. Yeats and Lionel Johnson had both brought out their separate
*Poems* in 1895; Ernest Dowson's *Verses* came out in 1896. And
Swinburne was still, of course, in full spate (*Astrophel and Other
Poems*, 1894; *A Tale of Balen*, 1896). With *A Shropshire Lad*
Housman in effect turned his back, ostentatiously and offensively,
on all that twaddle. Whereas the typical Romantic poem, from
"The Ancient Mariner" to "The Ballad of Reading Gaol," was
diffuse and repetitive, with occasional brilliant details but far too
often careless and slovenly, going on and on and on, a Housman
poem is short, precise, and the very reverse of slovenly in the details
of its poetic craftsmanship. It is true that Housman's poetry is still,
in the final analysis, "Romantic," but the concentration of style
in his best work obscures any underlying similarity by the exhil-
arating energy that is the immediate impression the reader obtains
from it. This difference is *primarily* attributable, I believe, to
Housman's exceptional susceptibility to the virtues of Latin.

The proposition has at any rate an *a priori* probability. I agree
that the Latin influence is not always immediately detectable. Housman himself once gave the chief "sources" of *A Shropshire Lad*
as "Shakespeare's songs, the Scottish Border Ballads, and Heine." [2]
To this list he might have added (i) the Authorized Version of the
Bible (which has contributed more phrases and idioms to his verse
than any other source), and (ii) the poems of Robert Louis Steven-
son, an early idol whose feet of clay he did not discover until much
later. But a literary source is not the same thing as a linguistic
influence. Housman's literary sense was acute—his undergraduate
years had after all been spent in the Oxford of Matthew Arnold

[2] Letter to Pollet.

and Walter Pater (though his own tutors at St. John's seem to have been dullards)—and he would not have needed to be told that both Greek literature and English literature were twice as good, considered simply as literature, as Roman literature. Norman Marlow, who has surveyed in some detail in his *A. E. Housman Scholar and Poet* (1958) all the literary sources hitherto reported, has only a few crumbs to record of direct Latin influence. The Mithridates who "died old" (*A Shropshire Lad*, lxii) is mentioned by both Martial and Juvenal because of the precautions he took to inure himself against poison by taking constant small doses. And there are also a few tags like "the sum of things" (*summa rerum;* not limited to Lucretius as Marlow states) which turn up from time to time.

The Latin "influence," by which I mean the influence of the Latin language on Housman's English, operated at a less conscious and much more fundamental level. A few elementary points are all that need to be made here. When Irwin complained in the lecture already referred to that "superfluity" was the besetting sin of English, he was thinking of Victorian English, of which this was certainly the grossest characteristic defect. More recent English prose and verse, even at its lower levels, has done something to correct the defect. Nevertheless Irwin's claim that Latin provides a model of "brevity" that an English writer can benefit from enormously still remains valid. This habit of verbal conciseness is probably Latin's most remarkable quality, and it is one that is inherent in the constitution of the language. It is possible, of course, to be verbose in Latin, but somehow even those Romans who achieved verbosity, as Cicero often did, managed it in fewer words than would be possible in any other European language. And Housman was not verbose. On the contrary, by utilizing a latent reserve of brevity in the Saxon basis of modern English, he was able to forge a style in English that challenges the verbal economy of Horace in Latin.

The critical problem, then, that is posed by Housman's best poems is the apparent union of two apparently incompatible qualities—a classic concision of style and a romantic extremism of temperament. I stress the *appearance* of both the union and the incompatibility, because the reality that lies behind the appearances is, I believe, neither strictly classical nor romantic. I shall call it *emphasis*, a stylistic quality that is inherent in Latin and difficult to attain in English without the artificial aids of italics or capital letters. Now emphasis was also the most prominent characteristic of Housman's personality. Whatever was said or done or suffered by this man surprises us by its excess. How on earth can so clever a man, the holder of a college scholarship who had obtained a First in the first part of Oxford's *lit. hum.* course, have failed *completely* in the second part ("Greats")? What quirk induced the London professor to adopt, not at all convincingly, the poetic *persona* of a Shropshire agricultural labourer? Why did Housman, the superbly skilful and sensitive emender of classical texts, find it necessary to adopt in his prose the controversial insolence of a Renaissance pedant? I ask these questions not to attempt to explain them but to illustrate the quality of personal excess in Housman of which "emphasis," my principal concern in this essay, was the stylistic expression in his writings.

The emphasis of the poems is best approached via the emphasis of the prose. Here is a characteristic passage from the preface to Housman's edition of the fifth book of Manilius (1930), which has the advantage of being detachable from its context and of being concerned with a modern English poem and not with a Latin one:

The following stanza of Mr. de la Mare's "Farewell" first met my eyes, thus printed, in a newspaper review.

Oh, when this my dust surrenders
Hand, foot, lip, to dust again,
May these loved and loving faces
Please other men!
May the rustling harvest hedgerow
Still the Traveller's Joy entwine,
And as happy children gather
Posies once mine.

I knew in a moment that Mr. de la Mare had not written *rustling*, and in another moment I had found the true word. But if the book of poems had perished and the verse survived only in the review, who would have believed me rather than the compositor? The bulk of the reading public would have been perfectly content with *rustling*,

nay they would sincerely have preferred it to the epithet which the
poet chose. If I had been so ill-advised as to publish my emendation,
I should have been told that *rustling* was exquisitely apt and poetical,
because hedgerows do rustle, especially in autumn, when the leaves
are dry, and when straws and ears from the passing harvest-wain
(to which "harvest" is so plain an allusion that only a pedant like
me could miss it) are hanging caught in the twigs; and I should
have been recommended to quit my dusty (or musty) books and make
a belated acquaintance with the sights and sounds of the English
countryside. And the only possible answer would have been *ugh!*"

This, it will be agreed, is emphatic prose. The quantity of
contemptuous disgust that Housman managed to pack into its
last sentence would have received the admiring approval of Juvenal
himself. The sarcasm of the long sentence preceding it is perhaps
less effective because the realistic details tend to obscure the conviction Housman wishes to enforce upon us that the bulk of the
reading public is an ass. But, of course, he was right. De la Mare
wrote *rusting* and not *rustling*. It is typical, however, of this kind of
criticism by emphatic assertion that Housman does not actually
give "the true word," or even provide any positive basis for preferring it. What disconcerts one in this case is that Housman relied
so exclusively on his own inner literary light that he did not take
the trouble to compare his newspaper's text with that in de la
Mare's *Collected Poems* of 1920, where "Fare Well" made its first
appearance in book-form, or even with that in such reputable
and easily available anthologies as *Georgian Poetry 1918–1919*
(1920) or J. C. Squire's *Selections from Modern Poets* (1921), both
of which print the poem. If he had done so he would have found
that his newspaper had committed a second misprint. De la Mare
did not write

> May *these* loved and loving faces . . .

but, in opposition to "this my dust" of the stanza's first line,

> May *those* loved and loving faces . . . (my italics)

The difference between knowing "in a moment" that *rustling*
was the wrong word and not realizing that *these* was also wrong is
the difference between one kind of emphasis and another: that of

what might be called the pictorial imagination and that of the logical sense. Housman was more adept, in other words, at making his opponent *look* a fool than at making him *prove* himself a fool.

It is pictorial emphasis too that predominates in Housman's poems. The recognition that de la Mare's "harvest hedgerow" must be *rusted* is a fellow-feeling for the same broad descriptive brush that he had himself used in the famous "coloured counties" of "In summertime on Bredon"; an even closer example of the same habit of generalized description is the later

> On acres of the seeded grasses
> The changing burnish heaves.

On the other hand, the introduction of "traveller's joy" in this poem (*Last Poems,* xl) is untypically detailed and the image may even have been lifted by him from de la Mare's "Fare Well."

Pictorial emphasis is common in the poems. The first stanza of "Reveille" (*A Shropshire Lad,* iv) is thoroughly Latin in its rhetorical elimination of realistic paraphernalia:

> Wake: the silver dusk returning
> Up the beach of darkness brims,
> And the ship of sunrise burning
> Strands upon the eastern rims.[3]

What I have called the illogical strain in Housman is also found in this poem in a transition from these baroque grandiosities (which are continued in the second verse) to the common day of "Up, lad, up, 'tis late for lying" with which the third verse begins. The indecorum of the transition results in a rather cheap over-emphasis. (The abrupter the descent from magnificence the more the reader sits up, but the descent must also justify itself aesthetically—as Housman's indecorousness often fails to do.)

The problem of Housman's emphatic vulgarities—which have nothing to do with the contemporary vulgarities of Kipling's *Bar-*

---

[3] An even more Latin opening stanza is to be found in *A Shropshire Lad,* x:

> The Sun at noon to higher air,
> Unharnessing the silver Pair
> That late before his chariot swam,
> Rides on the gold wool of the Ram.

*rack Room Ballads*—cannot be resolved without some further reference to Housman's private life. Indeed, the best poems are almost certainly the most personal ones, though the egotism is sometimes concealed. John Sparrow has already called attention to the special autobiographical significance of one of the poems published after Housman's death by his brother Laurence (*More Poems,* xxxiv):

> May stuck the land with wickets:
> For all the eye could tell,
> The world went well.

> Yet well, God knows, it went not,
> God knows, it went awry;
> For me, one flowery Maytime,
> It went so ill that I
> Designed to die.

> And if so long I carry
> The lot that season marred,
> 'Tis that the sons of Adam
> Are not so evil-starred
> As they are hard.

Mr. Sparrow has pointed out that in 1881, the year when Housman surprised Oxford by failing in Greats, the examination began on 28 May.[4] But the disaster that the poem records must surely have *preceded* the examination, which continued well into June. It seems more probable that the failure in Greats was the symptom or effect of some much more personal tragedy. When he was asked about the examination many years later by a colleague at Cambridge, Housman answered that the examiners had no option: "he showed up no answers to many of the questions set." [5] I take this to mean that the failure was a deliberate act, a part of the same mood of depression in which he had "Designed to die." Nobody with Housman's command of Latin and Greek could possibly have failed to scrape through Greats in 1881, when standards were decidedly lower than they are today, unless he had *wanted* to be ploughed.

[4] *Independent Essays* (London: Faber & Faber, 1963), pp. 140–41.
[5] A. S. F. Gow, *A. E. Housman: A Sketch* (London: Cambridge University Press, 1936), p. 7.

The personal tragedy is usually and probably rightly connected with his feelings for Moses Jackson, his one great Oxford friend in spite of the latter's being "a scientist and an athlete whose contempt for letters was unconcealed." [6] It is a reasonable guess that Jackson rejected Housman's homosexual advances with brutal finality that "flowery Maytime" of 1881:

> It irked you, and I promised
> To throw the thought away.

But Housman, who later remained on friendly terms with Jackson until the latter's death, then discovered that it was easier to contemplate suicide than to put it into practice. I take this episode to have been "the really emotional part" of his life. Its recollection in tranquillity more than ten years later was no doubt the efficient cause of *A Shropshire Lad,* though what he remembered was not only the rejection of love but his discovery that his own human heart was "hard," too hard to have really wanted to end it all by self-murder.

These speculations may help the sympathetic reader to get to critical grips with one of the most brilliant as well as one of the shortest poems in *A Shropshire Lad* (no. xvi):

> It nods and curtseys and recovers
> When the wind blows above,
> The nettle on the graves of lovers
> That hanged themselves for love.
>
> The nettle nods, the wind blows over,
> The man, he does not move,
> The lover of the grave, the lover
> That hanged himself for love.

There is not one superfluous word in this exquisite lyric. The last line of the second stanza is not, as a careless reading might suggest, a repetition of the first stanza's last line but a contrast to it; the plurals have become singulars. The lovers of the first stanza may have died together in a suicide pact, but the second stanza presents a solitary suicide, a single rejected or abandoned lover. Housman too had once been a lover of the grave in the sense that he had "designed" to hang himself when Jackson refused his love. But, in the more literal sense of a dead lover *in* the grave, one who had actually hanged himself for love, Housman can only salute this man who was not as "hard" as he had found himself to be.

> The man, he does not move.

What does move in the curiously abstract graveyard of Housman's imagination are the stinging nettles on the suicide's grave. In *More Poems*, xxxii, the nettle has become a general symbol of evil:

> It peoples towns, and towers
> About the courts of Kings,
> And touch it and it stings.

But in the *Shropshire Lad* poem the nettle seems to stand too for the gracefulness and resilience of a living object. In the series of verbs with which the poem opens—each verb one syllable longer than its predecessor as the force of the wind increases[7]—the nettle adjusts itself to the pressure of external circumstance by its mobility. Unlike the suicide who "does not move," who is finished physically, the nettle survives and in due course "the wind blows over." The parallel with Housman's own case is difficult to resist (he too was a stinging nettle by 1895), though any such an autobiographical interpretation must not be pressed too far. I am only calling attention to what seems to be implicit in the poem's imagery, to a level of personal meaning below the verbal surface.

The theme of suicide, particularly an unhappy lover's suicide, recurs so often in Housman's poems—with its variants of the deserter

---

[7] The *O.E.D.* cites this line under *recover* 21c to exemplify "To rise again after bowing or courtseying," but the only other example given is from *The Spectator*, December 5, 1711, where the word clearly refers to the movement forward *after* the "Town-Gentleman" "made a profound Bow and fell back, then recovered with a soft Air and made a Bow to the next, and so to one or two more. . . ." The interesting discussion of the poem by Randall Jarrell (p. 58) seems mistaken in saying "*nod* and *curtsey* and *recover* add up to *dance.*" The nettles remain rooted in the ground and so cannot be said to dance even metaphorically. Housman's "recovers" must be taken with the following line ("When the wind blows above"); the nettle returns to the vertical in a lull of the wind, so giving the appearance of nodding or curtseying.

who is shot or the murderer who is hanged—that the further possibility must be faced that he *exploited* in recollection the "emotional part" of his life. The insinuation of a degree of insincerity is part of the general thesis I have been presenting of this poetry of emphasis. The general pessimism may also come into the same category. If Housman's letter to his French admirer is to be believed he "became a deist at 13 and an atheist at 21." Well, an atheist does not curse "Whatever brute and blackguard made the world" (*Last Poems*, ix), because he knows that the world was not created supernaturally. And he is not disturbed by the thought that "high heaven and earth ail from the prime foundation" (*A Shropshire Lad*, xlviii) because he does not believe in either a high heaven or a prime foundation. In these poems Housman seems to be utilizing for merely rhetorical purposes a system of religion that he had abandoned long before he wrote them. Other examples will immediately suggest themselves to anybody familiar with Housman's poems.

An autobiographical core, even if increasing maturity has destroyed its personal relevance—or rather *provided that* some such process has occurred—is a *sine qua non* of this poetry of emphasis. The assumption justifies and excuses Housman's sentimental use of Shropshire place-names, including such errors of detail as the attribution of a steeple to the church at Hughley, because to a boy born and bred in Worcestershire, as Housman was, the Shropshire hills had once really been the western horizon where the sun set. A group of poems that may also have had some autobiographical content are those about soldiers. In Housman's London years the regiments quartered there normally provided middle-class homosexuals with their male prostitutes. The suggestion is a guess, but it is a guess that would help to explain his preoccupation with the lower ranks, especially in *A Shropshire Lad*. Indeed, the *persona* of the Shropshire yokel that holds the collection together may well derive from Housman's association with such men, most of whom were at that time country-born. If I am right, the soldier poems and such extensions from them as the pseudo-Pindaric "To an Athlete Dying Young" would acquire a new dimension from their personal implications.

## II

The poetry of emphasis of which Housman was a master can be compared to Latin poetry, but the thesis I have been propounding is not that it is especially like that of a particular Roman poet such as Propertius, his favourite. What I believe he tried to do, with considerable success, was to provide an English parallel to the Roman lyric by using the potentially emphatic elements in English for a somewhat similar purpose. The elements themselves, however, were naturally different, English being an uninflected language without the elaborate system of case-endings; "agreement" of adjective with noun; moods, tenses, and "persons" of the verb; grammatical genders, etc. that enabled Latin to achieve its special brevity and concentration. In their place Housman substituted three special characteristics of English speech—the monosyllable, a sort of internal rhyme, and the compound word.

Some statistics may be useful at this point. *A Shropshire Lad* has no five-syllable words at all. Apart from the hyphened compound words there are only seven four-syllable words in it, and with the same exception fifty-five three-syllable words. All the remaining words in the sixty-three poems are monosyllables or disyllables, and no less than twenty of the sixty-three poems have no words at all of more than two syllables. The number of words of Latin origin are therefore inevitably few and far between, though their effect when they do occur is proportionately great. In what is for me the most memorable poem in *A Shropshire Lad* ("Others, I am not the first," no. xxx) the best line is certainly the last,

> Beneath the suffocating night.

Here the combination of the four syllables of "suffocating" and the monosyllabic "night" clinches with memorable effect a poem made up entirely of emphatic monosyllables and disyllables—with the one exception of line 8, the midpoint of the poem, with its three-syllable latinism,

> Fear contended with desire.

Gerard Manley Hopkins's comment on Dryden ("his style and his rhythms lay the strongest stress of all our literature on the naked thew and sinew of the English language") is equally applicable to Housman. I am thinking now of some of the internal rhymes and half-rhymes, especially in *A Shropshire Lad,* which if it has more failures and vulgarities than *Last Poems* or the posthumous poems also has far more triumphs. Here are a few:

> His folly has not fellow
>> Beneath the blue of day . . .     (xiv)

and

> In the nation that is not
>> Nothing stands that stood before . . .     (xii)

and

> Eyes the shady night has shut
>> Cannot see the record cut . . .     (xix)

and

> A neck God made for other use
>> Than strangling in a string . . .     (ix)

Of the compound words much the most striking are the epithets, notably *sky-pavilioned* (iv), *valley-guarded* (xlii), *twelve-winded* (xxxii), *felon-quarried* (lix), *steeple-shadowed* (lxi)—all from *A Shropshire Lad*. The verbal economy of such compounds is here too a form of emphasis.

The reservation that must always be made with Housman—as with all but two or three of the Roman poets—is whether the stylistic brilliance has not been accompanied by a certain coarseness of human fibre. W. H. Auden's sonnet (reprinted on p. 11) has made the point in a brilliant image:

> Deliberately he chose the dry-as-dust,
> Kept tears like dirty postcards in a drawer . . .

Since the emotional part of his life ended when he was only twenty-two, did he perhaps have no tears to keep? Were the postcards hoarded because they came in useful for an artist in words who would otherwise have had nothing to write about? Is the emphasis just a little too emphatic?

The questions suggest themselves in Housman's case more insistently than with a Juvenal or a Lucan, two Latin masters of emphasis whom he was to edit, or indeed with any Latin poet, because of the reader's suspicion that Housman exploited in cold blood the emotional experiences of his youth and early manhood. What had been private and intimate has become public, too public; the emphasis is too self-regarding, too egotistical. Such suspicions may, however, be the price that a poet writing in English has to pay who tries to emulate the Roman *gravitas* ("weight") by using a concentration of monosyllables to provide an English equivalent to the verbal density that Latin possessed ready-made in its system of inflections. But these linguistic devices, when elevated from "language" to "style," work in opposite directions. When a Horace exploits the compactness of diction implicit in the inflectional system of Latin, the effect is to devulgarize his often commonplace subject-matter and in the process to dignify the poet as a human being. English monosyllables, on the other hand, because of their familiarity and trivial associations, tend to vulgarize and sentimentalize whatever experience they are used to describe.

The point can be illustrated over and over again from Housman's writings. By the side of "And the only possible answer would have been *ugh!*" from his prose we can set a couplet from "To an Athlete Dying Young":

> Eyes the shady night has shut
> Cannot see the record cut . . .

To "cut" or improve upon a record is a modern colloquialism that is not even listed in the *Oxford English Dictionary;* its presence here inevitably lowers the poem's heroic tone. The word is undeniably effective, but almost on the same level as *ugh*—emphatic but decidedly undignified. Unfortunately *A Shropshire Lad* considered as an aesthetic whole "wants" to achieve a dignified emphasis. It would not be true that Housman never achieves it. I think, for example, of xxxi:

> On Wenlock Edge the wood's in trouble;
> His forest fleece the Wrekin heaves . . .

(But "in trouble" only just escapes the emphasis of vulgarity.) And there is xl:

> Into my heart an air that kills
> From yon far country blows . . .

Here "kills" is a superbly emphatic monosyllable; but its effect is partly mitigated by the artificially archaic "yon." The knife-edge of monosyllables on which Housman's style is poised has on one side the words felt to be too colloquial (he overdoes *oh*, for example), and on the other side the words pretending to be rustic (*lad* is the worst offender, but there is also *lief*). The dilemma in a sense is one that every poet is in. "Words too familiar, or too remote," as Dr. Johnson put it in the life of Dryden, "defeat the purpose of a poet. From those sounds which we hear on small or on coarse occasions, we do not easily receive strong impressions or delightful images; and words to which we are nearly strangers, whenever they occur, draw that attention on themselves which they should transmit to things." For Housman, however, the common problem had become much more acute. Instead of having the whole of the English language to draw on in his poems he is virtually confined, because of his obsession with emphasis, to monosyllables occasionally varied with disyllables. And so, if he has finally to be dismissed as a minor poet of remarkable talent, the reason is perhaps primarily *technical*. The occasional cheap sentimentality and affected bitterness are effects rather than causes of the stylistic ambition to write English poems that would be *mutatis mutandis* more Latin even than those written by the Romans themselves. Housman might well have been a much better poet if he had been less expert in Latin. As it is, the Professor of Latin had the last word—in the excavation at Wroxeter (Uriconium):

> The tree of man was never quiet:
> Then 'twas the Roman, now 'tis I.

# "The Leading Classic of His Generation"

## by J. P. Sullivan

The intensely English cult of A. E. Housman as scholar, poet, and personality has proceeded beyond the check-list to the anthology; disregarding Housman's own injunction against collecting his scattered classical papers, Mr. Carter has presented us with all of Housman's continuous non-technical prose that is worth reading and some, such as a fragment from a paper on Arnold, that is not. Perhaps for the ceremonial addresses the *Praefanda* from *Hermes* might have been substituted to give us an example of Housman's Latin style and remind us of a side of Housman that did not let prudery interfere with the search for truth.

Opinions on his prose style will remain divided: "a prose, old-fashioned and elaborate, which somewhat resembles Pope's" was Edmund Wilson's comment, but an admirer of Housman, D. R. Shackleton Bailey, has called it "an agile, provocative, intensely personal style, partly deriving from Bentley's but with a closer affinity, I sometimes think, to Bernard Shaw's." The resemblance to the easy colloquial style of Bentley I myself cannot see, and the similarity to Shaw can only lie in its *épatant* tone. A brisker and less sonorous Macaulay would be my counter in this profitless game.[1] It is rather the *tone* of these pieces that is intriguing and for all the cultured references one is left with a vague uneasiness at the disproportionate emotion expended on Housman's textual predecessors. It is easy to see what elements in Housman's writing prompted Edmund Wilson to feel that here one was in the company of a very English mind which "has somehow managed to grow old without in a sense ever coming to maturity."

One can be grateful to the editor for more than Housman's style and the *Schadenfreude* his prefaces provide: here in a convenient form are most of Housman's thoughts on his profession and its proper aims. It is to this content that I propose to address myself. For the power of Housman's precept and practice is not confined to textual criticism, but extends over the whole field of classical study. It would not be too much to say that Housman's whole work is a representation in little of the theory and practice of English classical studies.

Academic England is as prone to snobbery as any other part of English life, and in Housman classicists have found an *arbiter elegantiae* of a most formidable sort. What was one man's choice of study, dictated by his own inclinations and his great if narrow talents, has been erected into a choice for a whole profession: his choice was "those minute and pedantic studies in which I am fitted to excel and which give me pleasure." Housman himself, it may be thought, was but negatively responsible for this: he had warned that "Everyone has his favourite study, and he is therefore disposed to lay down, as the aim of learning in general, the aim which his favourite study seems specially fitted to achieve, and the recognition of which as the aim of learning in general would increase the popularity of that study and the importance of those who profess it" (p. 2).

Housman was in fact confirming for his period the criteria of excellence which have dominated English classical studies since

---

[1] Cp., e.g., "In the vast field of criticism on which we are entering, innumerable reapers have already put their sickles. Yet the harvest is so abundant that the negligent search of a straggling gleaner may be rewarded with a sheaf" (Macaulay, "Essay on Milton"); and "skimming the first cream off a new-found author is only child's play beside gleaning after Bentley over a stubble where Heinsius has reaped" (Housman, "The Manuscripts of Propertius," Carter p. 90).

Bentley. Bentley—Porson—Housman, the tradition runs: these are the three luminaries of English classical studies, and these dictate the standards of classical prestige in Britain. Textual criticism is queen of classical studies, and those disciplines closest to it contend for the other places at court.

The four key documents for an understanding of Housman and his influence are the *Introductory Lecture* (1892), *The Application of Thought to Textual Criticism* (1921), *The Name and Nature of Poetry* (1933), and the biographical memoir of Arthur Platt (1927). Each of them raises issues of great importance, but one thing strikes the impartial reader immediately: "the absolute honesty in the pursuit of truth" (D. S. Robertson), the "fierce intellectual honesty which would neither condone nor extenuate" (A. Ker), these are by no means obvious qualities in the above pieces, and Housman himself described the first as "rhetorical and not wholly sincere."

Instead we meet with prejudiced and sometimes tendentious remarks or persuasive definitions which are still paraphrased by his admirers when criticising classical work which runs counter to the Housman tradition.

The *Introductory Lecture* ostensibly defends the Arts against the claims of Science. But the defence is not the personal or cultural benefits of humane studies, for Housman denies us any such responsibility, but the personal liberty of the Cyrenaic and the pragmatic value of any sort of truth. Knowledge is a good for man because it gives him pleasure and at most because "it must in the long run be better to see things as they are than to be ignorant of them." Any academic pursuits then which attract us personally have an equal claim on our attention and, by this reasoning, they should have equal honour in our universities. There is no conception of knowledge as an organized whole; there is no suggestion that some studies are more important or more valuable than others. Why certain literary studies, including classics, have a prestige not accorded to others is left unexplained. Prejudice and cant might be Housman's answer, for the humane benefits of academic classics seem negligible: few classical scholars get from their literary studies any just appreciation of literary excellence. This, according to Housman, requires congenital organs of literary perception, which are but rarely found and which may be stimulated by a small amount of classical training. Bentley is introduced as a prime example of a great scholar whose deficiency of taste is glaring:

> Turn what they will to Verse, their Toil is vain,
> Critics like me shall make it Prose again.

Ignoring Housman's view of the rarity of such organs of literary perception, which ties in with his romantic views on the rarity and nature of the true poet, one may see at once certain confusions in Housman's train of reasoning. To begin with, he seems to identify a classical training simply with the pursuit of knowledge, any sort of knowledge, and offers us the impression of a factual and almost scientific study. Secondly, he assumes that the study of classical literature, however pursued, is automatically a *literary* study; and so when certain practitioners like Bentley turn out defective in taste, he assumes that literary studies therefore cannot inculcate critical taste at all. This is not necessarily true, nor is the implication valid that Arnold's literary sense was refined by a very small amount of classical reading. Anyone who looks over Arnold's collected works will find there a self-education and a refining of method as rigorous as any. If Housman thought that Arnold's critical achievement was due to some divine natural gift, which required no training or hard work, he was mistaken.

Thirdly, Housman throughout the lecture assimilates humane studies to classical studies in England with their own particular tradition derived from Bentley. And it could be argued that this particular method of studying the classics does not "beautify our inner natures" because it is not meant to and is not suitable for such a purpose, not because humane studies cannot of their nature pass on any cultural advantages.

Much of what Housman says is reminiscent of certain remarks of Macaulay, but Macaulay's diagnosis is different. Macaulay does not, like Housman, subscribe to the thesis that the organs of literary perception are rarely found in a man, that these organs, if they exist, are easily stimulated or that literary criticism is some god-given faculty which rises like genius in unpredictable places and times. Macaulay says pertinently:

> At the time of the revival of literature, no man could, without

great and painful labour, acquire an accurate and elegant knowledge
of the ancient languages. And, unfortunately, those grammatical
and philological studies, without which it was impossible to understand the great works of Athenian and Roman genius, have a
tendency to contract the views and deaden the sensibility of those who
follow them with extreme assiduity. A powerful mind, which has
been long employed in such studies, may be compared to the gigan-
tic spirit in the Arabian tale, who was persuaded to contract himself
to small dimensions in order to enter within the enchanted vessel,
and when his prison had been closed upon him, found himself un-
able to escape from the narrow boundaries to the measure of which
he had reduced his stature. When the means have long been the
objects of application, they are naturally substituted for the end.
It was said by Eugene of Savoy, that the greatest generals have
commonly been those who have been at once raised to command, and
introduced to the great operations of war, without being employed
in the petty calculations and manoeuvres which employ the time
of an inferior officer. In literature the principle is equally sound, the
great tactics of criticism will, in general, be best understood by those
who have not had much practice in drilling syllables and particles. . . .

Of those scholars who have disdained to confine themselves to
verbal criticism few have been successful. The ancient languages
have, generally, a magical influence on their faculties. They were
"fools called into a circle by Greek invocations." The Iliad and
Aeneid were to them not books, but curiosities, or rather reliques.
They no more admired those works for their merits than a good
Catholic venerates the house of the Virgin at Loretto for its architec-
ture. Whatever was classical was good. Homer was a great poet; and
so was Callimachus. The epistles of Cicero were fine; and so were
those of Phalaris . . . (*On the Athenian Orators*).

Now whether Macaulay is entirely justified or not in his pessimism, at least he does not subscribe to Housman's view that just
literary perception is altogether rare. He rightly sees it in cultural
contexts, contexts of self-denial and self-stultification, however necessary such limitations were in the Renaissance. But both Housman
and Macaulay in their different ways support a later critic's contention that "the common result of a classical education is to incapacitate from literature for life." Whether the nature of classical

study is such that this is inevitable or whether our present methods of study are at fault is another question.

Not surprisingly Housman begs this question in the interest of his own tastes. He does not pause to consider whether Arnold, Lessing, and Goethe developed their faculties by any other study or whether in fact their study of classical *literature* may not have been as deep as his study of the classical tongues, but deep in a quite different way. Etymologists of English know much more about our language in one sense than many great writers, but it cannot be said that they know the language *better* than such writers or that they have worked harder at their studies. In effect, by deny-ing any humanistic responsibility, Housman elevates his own prac-tice into an ideal; it seems to follow that "the minute and accurate study of the classical tongues affords Latin professors their only excuse for existing." Yet this is neither obvious nor true, as the titles of many British chairs and faculties indicate (e.g., *Literae Humaniores* at Oxford and Professor of Humanity in Glasgow). Such titles look to other things as well, which should follow and complete "the minute and accurate study" which is admittedly a prerequisite for any classical teaching or research. Who would suggest that all professors of English be Germanic philologists or experts on Elizabethan printing like Mr. Fredson Bowers?

In Housman's statement there is a confusion between education and research. Housman's indifferentism, his defence of the study of whatever attracts the scholar, is tempting and research institu-tions wisely follow this line; there is, however, no justification for its imposition on a system of education, for forcing the young to study literary texts in a way that attracts *us*.

Of course, Housman could weep over *Diffugere nives* and claim that it was the greatest poem in the language, and in private teach-ing no doubt literary judgments are made and offered to our pupils, but as serious literary discussion is not encouraged in our subject, there is no discipline and thus no check on the possible irresponsibility of such literary comment. The "watery" or the "dry" alternate in the education we offer. And it is only occasionally when some poor scholar unwittingly goes beyond his last and ventures to offer some literary comment on his author that we see the truth of Housman's remarks on the absolute poverty of literary comment by the trained classicist. The main disagreement with Housman centers on his inference that no training is possible or desirable even for those who have some native aptitude for literature. No one can become an artist without great native ability and some like the Douanier Rousseau and Grandma Moses have managed without training, but are art schools and artistic apprenticeships therefore useless?

Housman remarks: "The majority of mankind, as is only natural, will be most attracted by those sciences which most nearly concern human life; those sciences which, in Bacon's phrase, are drenched in flesh and blood . . . The men who are attracted to the drier . . . sciences, say logic or pure mathematics or textual criticism, are likely to be fewer in number; but they are not to suppose that the comparative unpopularity of such learning renders it any the less worthy of pursuit." Of course not, nor any the more worthy. But our attempt to impose, as a standard pattern, our own drier preferences on the education which we offer not only molds those who desire to excel in our subject and so perpetuates the tradition, but drives many students of equal intelligence and different aptitudes into subjects where their contribution to the common pursuit can be more profitably made. In Oxford, for instance, they betake themselves to logical analysis or epigraphy or some similar subject which bears a greater relation to the name and nature of philosophical and historical studies than textual criticism and the other ancillary studies do to the study of classical literature.

Housman's indifferentism is valid only if we think of personal satisfaction. By all means we should follow the direction of our aptitudes, but it is absurd to suggest, as Housman does, that there is no difference in value between one department of learning and another. This is not to deny the seeming fairmindedness of one of his concluding remarks. He remarked "we can all dwell together in unity without crying up our own pursuits or depreciating the pursuits of others on factitious grounds."

Some of the thoughts in *The Application of Thought to Textual Criticism* partly explain the honour paid to current philological practice. Housman, for all his own professed enjoyment, rather underestimates the pleasures of textual criticism and kindred studies: the delight in the limited problem satisfactorily solved with some approach to finality, the pleasure in bringing to bear a number of techniques and items of knowledge, the visual pleasures of palaeography, the ease of formulation, the multitude of guides, predecessors, and advisors, the acceptability of the pursuit, its fertility in learned papers—all these adequately compensate for the rarity with which nowadays one's emendations are admitted to the text or one's vulnerability to superior scholars like Housman. Were textual criticism and exegesis *not* so pleasant (and prestigious), why would so many scholars be engaged in them? Why would there be so many articles and books containing nothing but textual notes and explications published, often when a full commentary is lacking on a certain author? This last, of course, requires a treatment of *all* the problems, not just the more soluble and congenial difficulties.

Housman however remarks, moderately enough, "It has sometimes been said that textual criticism is the crown and summit of all scholarship. This is not evidently or necessarily true; but it is true that the qualities which make a critic, whether they are thus transcendent or no, are rare, and that a good critic is a much less common thing than, for instance, a good grammarian" (p. 133).

This rarity of the good critic (although at this time Housman was claiming for him little more than reason and commonsense) has imperceptibly led to the attribution to him of almost superhuman qualities. Consider, for example, a recent remark made to the same body as Housman was addressing, the Classical Association, by the distinguished editor of Ovid, Mr. E. J. Kenney:

> The editing of a classical text is a discipline that calls forth the widest possible range of knowledge and the richest possible combination of talents. The greatest practitioners of the past have been among the giants of scholarship.

The logical questions of definition we may leave aside but we should notice at least the high ambition of our studies that rigorously encourages only the widest possible range of knowledge and the richest possible combination of talents. Mr. Kenney's remark is similar to Housman's description of emending and judging emendations: "To read attentively, think correctly, omit no relevant consideration, and repress self-will, are not ordinary accomplishments; yet an emendator needs much besides: just literary perception, congenial intimacy with the author, experience which must have been won by study, and mother wit which he must have brought from his mother's womb" (Pref. to Manilius V, p. 51). And as historians and philosophers require emendations too we may add to the critic's equipment a sound knowledge of historical probability and history and an interest in philosophical problems and a feeling for the ways philosophers think.

Housman himself however refutes this idea of the critic by his own remarks on Bentley. Bentley would cut up into four critics like Housman and Housman refers to his "unique originality and greatness" (p. 121), but he also speaks of "Bentley's firm reliance on his own bad taste" and describes him as "this tasteless and arbitrary pedant."

Taste then is not such a necessary part of the critic's equipment in practice, even though it may be theoretically of advantage. And in Bentley's case Housman was careful not to go as far as Housman's admirers go in discussing *him*. Housman rightly confessed he was no literary critic, but did regard himself as a connoisseur —"I think I can tell good from bad in literature." And eulogizers such as Percy Withers and D. S. Robertson describe him as "exquisitely sensitive to literary values" or refer to "the sureness of his aesthetic judgment." His one venture into literary criticism ("referring opinions to principles and setting them forth so as to command assent," as he defines it) will be examined later, but his claims to aesthetic judgment may be disposed of immediately. His taste was narrow and closely connected with the sort of poetry he wrote. Even within this range it was faulty. And although it was a definite taste, neither in his Manilius nor his Juvenal nor his Lucan can one see much scope for it or for that "congenial" intimacy with an author that he regarded as a prerequisite for the emendator. Satire he classed with controversy and burlesque in *The Name and Nature of Poetry*; of Lucan he said "his vocabulary is as commonplace as his diction." Manilius was "a facile and frivolous poet," and the *Ibis* was Ovid's best work.

Prose he does not seem to have cared much for: so one might infer from his favorite authors. *Cranford* he described as "one of the nicest stories ever written." Other preferences were Sinclair

Lewis, Theodore Dreiser, Edith Wharton, Anita Loos' *Gentlemen Prefer Blondes,* Josh Billings, and Artemus Ward. Mark Twain he liked, but Henry James he read "with some affliction at his prolixity." His favorite English novelist was Thomas Hardy. His favorite English poet was originally Matthew Arnold, but he read Edgar Allen Poe (!), "got more enjoyment from Edna St. Vincent Millay than from either Robinson or Frost"; Robert Bridges' *Shorter Poems* he called "the most perfect single volume of verse ever published"; William Watson's *Wordsworth's Grave* was "one of the precious things of English literature" and Masefield's plays "are well worth reading and contain a lot that is good."

All this may have the individuality of a poet's taste but even within these limits it is surely difficult to talk with conviction of his "just literary perception" in preferring Millay to Frost or finding much merit in Poe (cf. his remarks on Poe's *The Haunted Palace,* p. 187). But the real insight into his literary judgments may be obtained from his notorious comments on Milton and Shakespeare in the *Introductory Lecture* (p. 10 ff.). And that this was no attempt to be merely shocking seems confirmed by a witness who reports: "I have heard him say that it gave him no pleasure to read a play of Shakespeare's from beginning to end, for though some parts were magnificent, there were others so slovenly that the effect of the whole was disagreeable."

It is now becoming clear what sort of taste this is. On one hand a belief in something like Valéry's *poésie pure* which may or may not be pure nonsense (cf. his remarks on a perfectly understandable song of Shakespeare's—*Take o take those lips away,* p. 189); on the other a very "classical" preoccupation with form which leads him to say of Milton: "The dignity, the sanity, the unfaltering elevation of style, the just subordination of detail, the due adaptation of means to ends, the high respect of the craftsman for his craft and himself, which ennoble Virgil and the great Greeks, are all to be found in Milton, and nowhere else in English literature are they all to be found." Such remarks perhaps indicate why he says practically nothing of the poets of the post-war generation in England and seems scarcely to have known them: Eliot he seems to have approved of for writing sensibly on the poetry of *A Shropshire Lad.* A piece of adulation by A. Ker in the Memorial Edition of *The*

*Bromsgrovian* is an adequate commentary on this taste by another classicist: "There is no doubt that Housman's sober attention to form he owed to his classical reading; and in an age in which neglect of form seems the first requirement of a poet, he is likely to be discredited. . . . It may well be that the lyric poets of the future, looking for these things in vain among the coteries of the twentieth century, will turn for their touchstone of literary merit, to the poetry of Housman." *That* could only have been written by a classicist. The common element in Housman's literary judgments and such remarks as this from his admirers is what called forth once from a critic of classical education the following: "The common result of a classical training (need it be said that there are, of course, exceptions) is to incapacitate from contact with literature for life. . . . The resulting 'taste,' 'judgment' and 'sense of fitness' (usually so strong in the 'classic') are almost insuperable bars to the development of critical sensibility. For the 'classic,' Form is something that Flecker . . . has and Mr. Pound in *Hugh Selwyn Mauberley* most certainly hasn't" (F. R. Leavis, *Education and the University*, pp. 134–35).

Wisely then Housman disavows the title of literary critic in *The Name and Nature of Poetry*. Housman's conception of a literary critic is even more exalted than his or Mr. Kenney's conception of the textual critic (perhaps that is why one is a little shocked to find him mentioning Sir Walter Raleigh and A. C. Bradley in the same breath, p. 109):

"Whether the faculty of literary criticism is the best gift that Heaven has in its treasuries I cannot say; but Heaven seems to think so, for assuredly it is the gift most charily bestowed" (p. 168), and he says of Arthur Platt, "He knew better than to conceive himself that rarest of all the great works of God, a literary critic" (p. 158).

Goethe, Lessing, and Arnold, these are the mortals he admits to the literary pantheon as he put Scaliger, Bentley, Nicolaus Heinsius, and others into his textual pantheon. But whereas the second, for all the aptitudes requisite in a textual critic, is allowed a goodly number of adequate scholars, the literary critic must be supreme or nowhere. The journeymen of classics must be scholars in Housman's sense or nothing. This deference to the heights of criticism is accompanied by sneers at anything else—"the usual flummery of the cobbler who is ambitious to go beyond his last." Of Platt he says, "he stuck to business as a scholar should, and preferred, as a man of letters will, the dry to the watery." What exactly the scholar's last is, whether he be good cobbler or indifferent botcher, is clear from his remark to Platt that if he preferred one poet to another, then he was no true scholar.

*The Name and Nature of Poetry* is a strange but interesting document. It is valuable chiefly for the light it throws on Housman's taste and principles. One Cambridge critic lamented that it would take twelve years to undo the harm Housman had done in an hour. This is overestimating the influence of the classical scholar in the world of letters and Housman could do no harm to the criticism of classical authors: *cantabit vacuus coram latrone viator.*

Housman admits in this lecture that the good literature of several languages read for pleasure might do some good to the reader, "must quicken his perception though dull, and sharpen his discrimination though blunt, and mellow the rawness of his personal opinions." This is different stuff from what was implied in the *Introductory Lecture* about the effect of a classical education on those who lack the organs of literary perception. The contradiction is not formal but implicit.

In discussing poetry Housman's tendency towards persuasive definitions is as noticeable as in his definitions of the scholar and the literary critic. For Housman, as usual except in his textual work, is presenting a case or justifying a set of prejudices. Half the seventeenth and the eighteenth century are dismissed as almost barren of poetry in the highest sense, the latter on the extraordinary ground that the poetry of that age "differed in quality . . . from the poetry of all those ages, whether modern or ancient, English or foreign, which are acknowledged as the great ages of poetry." We soon see why. "Poetry is not the thing said but a way of saying it. Can it then be isolated and studied by itself? For the combination of language with its intellectual content, its meaning, is as close a union as can well be imagined. Is there such a thing as pure unmingled poetry, poetry independent of meaning? . . . Even when poetry has a meaning, *as it usually has* [my italics], it may well be inadvisable to draw it out. . . . *The Haunted Palace* is one of Poe's best poems so long as we are content to swim in the sensations it evokes and only vaguely to apprehend the allegory. . . . Meaning is of the intellect, poetry is not" [2] (p. 187). We soon find what poetry is of—"Poetry indeed seems to me more physical than intellectual." Housman offers a set of physical reactions as a touchstone: that such reactions might be built up artificially by non-poetical feelings such as sentiment or familiarity he never considers. Obviously such feeling could be roused by cheap as well as good poetry. Like the mystic who *knows* he has seen God and cannot understand why his apprehension is not accepted as veridical by the rest of the world, Housman puts his faith in this purely personal criterion and shows how his vaunted taste can be stimulated by the tumpty-tump follies of Poe as well as by the songs of Shakespeare.

If, as seems clear, Housman's acquaintance with classical literature did not give him that fine aesthetic taste which is sometimes claimed for him, it must also be added that his acquaintance in general with the ancient world seems to have given him only that illiberal set of prejudices which the world associates with a certain type of headmaster, although these may be in part due to what Shackleton Bailey calls his lack of "aptitude for broad generalization or for the arrangement of masses of uncoordinated material." In a letter to Laurence Housman, he asserted "civilization without slavery is impossible" and his brother glosses this as follows: "In politics he stayed aloof, over the benefit of a democratic government being a complete sceptic. He even believed that slavery was essential to a well-governed state, but was so English in his preference that he probably considered England a better-governed country under democratic mismanagement than any other favoured with a form of despotism of which, theoretically, he more greatly approved." Such remarks, from a professed admirer of Arnold, incidentally, seem to point to a complete isolation from life and a fundamental lack of that historical sense which a classical education is sometimes supposed to provide.

His biographical notice of Arthur Platt (pp. 154–60) allows us to see most clearly into the heart of the matter, although perhaps there

---

[2] It is, of course, obvious that such a belief in poetry as nonsense could not be applied to Latin poetry, for then the textual critic would have to acquiesce in some very strange things.

is no key to Housman's character which can be cut entirely from his conscious motives and expressed views.[3] The piece on Platt is interesting; it is a sort of Grammarian's Funeral Oration and the subtle differences from the ethos of Browning's poem are well worth study. The remarks on Platt's scholarship and personality are generous and two of the comments in particular are illuminating for the light they throw on Housman:

"In literary comment he did not expatiate, although, or rather because, he was the most lettered scholar of his time. He stuck to business, as a scholar should, and preferred, as a man of letters will, the dry to the watery. He knew better than to conceive himself that rarest of all the works of God, a literary critic; but such remarks on literature as he did let fall were very different stuff from the usual flummery of the cobbler who is ambitious to go beyond his last" (p. 158). And: "Nor were his studies warped and narrowed by ambition. A scholar who means to build himself a monument must spend much of his life in acquiring knowledge which for its own sake is not worth having and in reading books which do not in themselves deserve to be read . . ." (p. 159). The judgment of value implicit in this last statement, so at odds with the views of the *Introductory Lecture,* is not my concern here; the real significance lies in the overt ambition it exudes. This, taken in conjunction with the earlier dogmatic definition of the scholar's function in the same piece—grammar, metrics, exegesis, and textual criticism—explains much of Housman's theory and practice as well as the awed language he uses when talking of Bentley, the references to *lucida tela diei* and the adaptation of Arnold's description of Goethe, the physician of the Iron Age, to the healer of corrupt texts. This was Housman's own *métier.*

The energy which classical scholars have failed to devote to the nice discrimination of good and bad in the authors they study is usually spent on the nice discrimination in private of the merits and soundness of other scholars. Housman was no exception, and there is something egregiously childish in the prefaces with their

---

[3] A more penetrating analysis, based on intuition and gossip, is to be found in W. H. Auden's sonnet on Housman, omitted from his collected shorter poems, no doubt because of one line which is admittedly in bad taste. [Restored in 1967; see p. 11.]

mannered weighing of each critic's contribution to a text; on Bentley's *Manilius* he wrote "Haupt alone has praised it in proportion to its merit. . . . Had Bentley never edited *Manilius*, Nicolaus Heinsius would be the foremost critic of Latin poetry; but this is a work beyond the scope of even Heinsius. Great as was Scaliger's achievement, it is yet surpassed and far surpassed by Bentley's; Scaliger at the side of Bentley is no more than a marvellous boy" (p. 28). And examples might be multiplied.

Such praise of critics like Bentley naturally reflects glory on Housman's chosen line of study and Housman's own talents. Housman's genius was not for exploration, and he made nothing like the contribution of a Lachmann to textual science nor did he add a tithe of what, say, Milman Parry has added to our understanding of ancient literature. But in this matter reputation is not judged by impressive results or by large contributions to knowledge but by conformity to certain accepted criteria, criteria which Housman backed with the full force of his scholarly personality. Housman is offered to us as the model of the classical scholar, witness the eulogies I quoted earlier of the textual critic. Housman's ambition chose to build its monument in the narrow area where stand the monuments of Bentley and Porson and the smaller brasses of the English school of textual criticism. This is a closed world and within it the laudatory descriptions of its luminaries might be pardonably regarded by an outsider as appropriate only for some of our greatest English thinkers—*lucida tela diei* surely fits a Newton better than a Bentley. But a skillful walling off of classical reputation and scholarship from all comparison with other branches of study has produced some strange forced flowers of pride and reputation. The traditional regard for classical studies as a humane education bolsters this pride, even though the basis of that regard has passed away and the time has gone when our claims to intellectual merit were open to disinterested evaluation by more general criteria. Just as *we* cannot know what enormously high textual talents have been displayed in the study of Vedic texts, so the republic of letters cannot appreciate the high talents displayed in textual criticism of the classics nor evaluate this high intelligence and its contribution to culture. And of course by various self-denying ordinances no classical scholar has ever dared set himself up simultaneously as a man of letters and a great scholar—or if he has, he has never succeeded in impressing his peers in either field. It is this artificial situation which has to be taken into account when discussing Housman, and he should be set, not simply or solely in the context of classical studies, but in the context of a wider humane culture. Only then can an adequate evaluation of his contribution to the sum of things be made.

My object in the above has not been to disparage Housman's great talents, industry, and achievements as an editor and critic, but to define as clearly as possible his limitations as a model for all classical scholars. Not all have his talents nor should all borrow his prejudices. The cult of Housman sometimes seems an example of that "servile worship of eminent men and the irrational dread of innovation" which has at times been such a curse in classical studies, in Germany and the English-speaking countries, and which entailed, for example, such grudging recognition of the work of Milman Parry and such a stifling of free discussion in certain German Universities at certain periods. But this is not the main danger, which is rather a lack of proportion, a provinciality in our studies, which may cut them off from any new life and growth and ultimately extinguish any cultural value they might have. W. B. Stanford once said: "Some have thought . . . that the post-Bentleian tendency to make textual criticism the most honored form of classical scholarship weakened the humanistic tradition"; it has been perhaps our great misfortune that in a critical period for classical studies, in a time of educational change and reform, Housman with his considerable talents and equally considerable influence should have added his weight to an already powerful tendency. He thus created within our literary studies a strange rarefied atmosphere of intellectual snobbery and so prevented the development within classics of a literary discipline which would produce not simply more scholars and textual critics but educated men. As is obvious, Housman is not entirely to blame for this, but around his memory in the last twenty-five years or so have crystallized the attitudes of which I complain. And if anyone should think that my criticisms are exaggerated he has only to consider one devoted follower of Housman, D. R. Shackleton Bailey, who recently asked himself on the radio "what it is that has made my readings of the Manilius the most memorable intellectual experience of my life. . . ." This from a literate scholar living in the century of Freud, Einstein and Wittgenstein and conversant with a literature that produced Thucydides, Plato, and Aristotle!

# The Housman Dilemma

## by John Sparrow

"And my executor shall destroy without exception all my un-published MSS."—that well-worn testamentary injunction raises an issue as old as the *Aeneid,* and the considerations on either side—the sacredness of a dying author's wishes, as against the duty to literature, to posterity—are familiar and nicely balanced. On the death of A. E. Housman the old problem arose in a new and complicated form. The story is a tangled one, and it may be worth while to set it out in some detail.

Housman's brother Laurence was, by his will, permitted "to select from my verse manuscript writing and to publish any poems which appear to him to be completed and to be not inferior in quality to the average of my published poems," and directed "to destroy all other poems and fragments of verse." Mr. Laurence Housman made, and published, his selection from the four poetical notebooks left by A.E.H., and then, as the will directed, destroyed all leaves that contained nothing but unpublished matter. There remained a number of leaves carrying on one side drafts (in varying stages of finish) of published poems, and on the other side jottings and fragmentary drafts of poems which A.E.H. did not publish and which his brother decided were not worthy of publication. He was

"The Housman Dilemma" by John Sparrow. This review of Tom Burns Haber's *The Manuscript Poems of A. E. Housman* (Minneapolis: University of Minnesota Press; London: Oxford University Press, 1955) appeared in *The Times Literary Supplement,* April 29, 1955. It was reprinted in John Sparrow, *Controversial Essays* (New York: The Chilmark Press; London: Faber & Faber, 1966), pp. 71–84. Copyright *The Times Literary Supplement,* 1955. Reprinted by permission of *The Times Literary Supplement*; John Sparrow; the Chilmark Press; and Faber & Faber. Quotations from *The Manuscript Poems* by permission of the University of Minnesota Press.

anxious to preserve the first, but felt himself in duty bound to destroy the second.

In this situation, Mr. Laurence Housman should surely have made up his mind one way or the other. If he held his brother's wishes paramount, he should have destroyed all unpublished fragments, even if that involved sacrificing in the process drafts of published poems. If, on the other hand, he thought that the interests of literature required that those wishes should be disregarded, he should have preserved everything. Had he taken the second course he would have had his critics; but, right or wrong, he could have looked them squarely in the face.

Instead, Mr. Housman pursued a middle course. From the ambiguous leaves he cut away such portions as bore on both sides unpublished matter: and then, erasing or overscoring in ink or pencil everything, or almost everything, that had not already seen print, he pasted the remaining leaves and parts of leaves on to folio sheets so as to expose to view only the texts of poems which A.E.H., or he himself, had published.

In this unsatisfactory condition the manuscripts were sold to an American purchaser, the right to publish any still unpublished material being reserved to the author's estate. Nothing had been done to remove this restriction when the manuscripts passed by gift to the Library of Congress in 1940. In 1945 the Library authorities removed the leaves from the sheets on which they were pasted, and remounted them with hinges, so that the erased and cancelled texts on the versos were again exposed to view. This was done not with a view to publication but solely in order the better to preserve the manuscripts, on which the adhesive material was said to be having a deleterious effect. It was in 1947 that Mr. Tom Burns Haber, of Ohio State University, began to interest himself in the material thus made accessible, and during the summers of 1950, 1951, and 1952 he set to work deciphering what Mr. Laurence Housman had taken such pains to hide, and announced his intention of publishing his results. At this stage, protests were made in *The Times Literary Supplement* about Mr. Haber's project. Was it possible to stop the publication of the unpublished jottings and fragments by legal action? If so, who had the right to stop it? And—legal objections apart—was it, morally, right so to disregard the wishes of the poet and frustrate the evident intentions of his brother, through whom the manuscripts had been acquired?

It appears that, if objection had been taken and persisted in, it would have been possible to stop the publication by action in the Courts; for Mr. Haber, writing in answer to his critics in the *Literary Supplement* on 7 November 1952, declared, "All legal objections to this project have now been withdrawn"; and he says again, in his preface to the present book: "All legal objections have been withdrawn, in writing, by Laurence Housman and Barclay's Bank, the designated trustees." Exactly how this withdrawal of objection was secured, Mr. Haber does not tell us; nor does he tell anything of Mr. Laurence Housman's attitude in the matter at any stage. Mr. Housman himself, however, has left the public in no doubt about his feelings; writing to the *Oxford Mail* on 3 March 1955, he says:

> I made the great mistake of thinking that any manuscripts lodged at the Library of Congress would be treated with the same respect as those which I also lodged at the British Museum; and for that reason I failed to take the commercial precaution of securing the copyright. Had I done so none of these deplorable quotations could have been published.

These remarks are in more than one respect misleading: Mr. Housman did not "lodge" the manuscripts in the Library of Congress, and no step on his part was necessary in order to "secure" a copyright which was already his—and which, it seems, he must at some stage have surrendered to the Library or to Mr. Haber. However this may be, it seems clear that if he surrendered his rights, Mr. Housman regretted having done so: and it seems equally clear that Mr. Haber was aware of this in November 1952. By then, however, it was too late for Mr. Housman to retract, and Mr. Haber evidently intended to show him no mercy: for after announcing, in the letter already quoted, that legal objections had been withdrawn, he continued as follows:

> There remains the ethical objection. This received its final answer

when the persons standing nearest to the documents decided to preserve them and negotiated their sale. This was a sane and sensible decision, at which few will cavil. *Nescit vox missa reverti.*

After this unkindly taunt, he observed somewhat cryptically:

> Finally it is to be hoped that those who knowingly risked censure in handling the manuscript as they did will not at this late date shrink from the consequences of their choice; certainly they need not join in the chorus of dissent. Their decision was as right as it is irrevocable.

It looks as if the Library authorities had expressed misgivings which Mr. Haber was anxious to allay. If so, he was, it seems, successful; for the present opinion of the Library, he assures us in his preface to this volume, is that the publication "involves no ethical consideration which might 'embarrass the strictest sense of scholarly propriety.' "

We will leave it to the common reader to form his own conclusions about the "scholarly propriety" of these proceedings and to pass judgment as he thinks fit on the actors in the sorry drama, adding only that Mr. Haber says no word about this part of the story in the otherwise very full "History" of the manuscripts which forms Part One of the book under review.

"Otherwise very full": but there is one remarkable omission. In quoting the all-important clause in Housman's will—"And I permit him but do not enjoin him to select from my verse manuscript writing and to publish any poems which appear to him to be completed and to be not inferior in quality to the average of my published poems, *and I direct him to destroy all other poems and fragments of verse*"—Mr. Haber omits, and omits only, the words we have italicized. He quotes in full the order (though it is not strictly relevant to his purpose) to destroy all *prose* manuscripts, and it is to this that a reader might well think he is referring on the single occasion when he mentions an "order for destruction"; but nowhere in his book is the crucial direction of the testator to destroy unpublished poetical texts quoted or even paraphrased. Readers can draw their own conclusions about the reason for this strange omission.

Candour is the first quality of a true scholar; and surely Mr. Haber would have done better to say explicitly that A. E. Housman had prohibited, and (if such was the fact) that his brother deplored, what had been, and was being, done, but that the editor was undertaking his tasks in the interests of poetry and criticism.

Is poetry, or is criticism, in fact the richer for the publication of this matter? Housman's reputation, probably, will neither gain nor lose by what is now revealed. Here and there is a line or two of characteristic and not unworthy poetry:

> Haste for the heaven is westered since you came:
> Day falls, night climbs, the hour has lost its name;
> Quick, quick! the lightning's pace were weary, slow,
> And here you loiter spelling gravestones: go.

and, in a less familiar vein:

> Some air that swept the Arabian strand
> When the great gulf was calm,
> Some wind that waved in morning land
> The plumage of the palm.

But most of the jottings are no more than chips from the author's workshop, stamped with his character, and sometimes even reading like parodies of his style. Many, no doubt, are transcripts of those *vers donnés* that came into his head, as he explained in *The Name and Nature of Poetry*, without any conscious effort of composition on his part. No one will judge him by them, for better or for worse. But his admirers, and not only they, will be interested to observe how often a solitary line or stanza, years after its first transcription, was worked into a poem so perfectly that no reader of the completed whole would suspect its independent origin.

More interesting than fragments of abortive poems are the abandoned variants in the text of poems familiar in *A Shropshire Lad* and *Last Poems*, revealing as they do the poet's first and second, even his fifth and sixth, thoughts, his touchings and re-touchings, his repeated refining of his gold. One stanza of the last piece in *A Shropshire Lad* he had to rewrite (he tells us in *The Name and Nature*) thirteen times; the manuscript of that particular piece is not preserved, but the notebooks afford plenty

of analogous examples. The changes seem to have been almost
always for the better and the comparison is always of interest. It
is a pity that Mr. Haber has given only a small selection of the
variants in the text of published poems; the temptation to call
his book *The Manuscript Poems of A. E. Housman*—a misleading
hardly, indeed, an accurate, title—and the desire to present "Eight
Hundred Lines of Hitherto Uncollected Verse" was no doubt too
strong for him. His book therefore in the main consists of a mass
of what he correctly describes as "workshop material" which has
not yet, in any form, been exposed to the public view.

The presentation of this material is a work which, if it was
worth doing, was worth doing well. Indeed, work of this kind,
above all others, needs to be done scrupulously well if it is to be
done at all. What are the attributes that are needed for the
task? They are not many and not rare ones: patience to disentangle and rearrange the material; an eye capable of reading so
much of the text as is decipherable; accuracy in transcribing it
where it is clear; a becoming humility, where it is doubtful; and
an ear so attuned to the poet's voice that it can tell, where
the eye is defeated, what he must, or might, or could not possibly,
have written. Perhaps it is not unreasonable also to ask that an
editor of Housman should be capable of understanding Latin and
of writing English.

Of these attributes Mr. Haber has none, in any adequate degree, except the first. He has patiently reconstructed out of the
materials before him as much as remains of A.E.H.'s four poetical
notebooks; but he is sadly deficient in the power of seeing what
his author wrote and of transcribing accurately what he sees: he
lacks the intellectual humility that confesses the doubtfulness of
a doubtful reading; and he is patently deaf to the tones of Housman's voice.

Three or four stanzas will afford at once a further indication
of the poetical quality of the material with which Mr. Haber is
dealing, and of his competence to deal with it. On page 33 of his
book Mr. Haber prints the following quatrain, written in manuscript, "in pencil, beneath wavy cancellation in pencil":

> As often under sighing oak
> drowsing
> Or near musing hidden laid
> Maiden and youth in whispers spoke,
> In whispers, youth and maid.

"If there are reasonable grounds for conjecture in the reading of an erased or cancelled section," says Mr. Haber, "my reading is given, followed by an interrogation sign and enclosed in brackets." Can it really be that Mr. Haber did not think that "hidden," which makes nonsense of line 2, was a sufficiently doubtful reading to deserve an "interrogation sign"? Would not three minutes' thought have suggested to him that "linden" (under sighing oak—near musing linden) was more probably the right reading? But "thought" as Housman himself once observed, "is irksome, and three minutes is a long time"; neither his eye nor his ear suggested to Mr. Haber that anything was wrong with "hidden," and he prints it without any sign of misgiving.

On the next page Mr. Haber prints the couplet ("faded ink, beneath wavy cancellation in ink"):

> Never, or ever, shine or snow,
> That son of God I used to know.

Did it not occur to Mr. Haber, on grounds of sense and sound, that Housman must, or (to say the least) might, have written not "or ever" but "o never"? Or can it be that what is hidden by the "wavy cancellation" is so clearly "or ever" that "o never" did not deserve to be suggested, even as a possible alternative?

On page 42 is the following: "erased" in the manuscript "and cancelled with pencil wave":

> Heard in the hour of pausing voices,
> That brings the turning wheel to stand,
> When barges moor and windows glisten,
> And lights are faded in the land.

Mr. Haber obligingly provides a facsimile of the page on which this quatrain was written. Judging from the facsimile alone, one would say that "fasten" and not "glisten" is the last word in line 3; certainly to print "glisten" with not even a sign of interrogation is a dereliction of editorial duty. The superiority of "fasten" has been pointed out in print elsewhere;[1] "glisten," though not impossible, is inferior both in meaning and in sound. Even if Mr. Haber's ear and his intelligence did not tell him that "fasten" was the better reading, his eye should have perceived that it ought at any rate to be recorded as an alternative.

On page 54 is the following characteristic couplet, found in the manuscript "beneath wavy cancellation":

> Better to think your friend's unkind
> Than know your lover's untrue.

Is the "cancellation" so ineffective that Mr. Haber can be certain that Housman wrote "lover's" in line 2? And even if he wrote "lover's," must not "love's" have been what he intended? In either alternative, to print "lover's" without a note or a question-mark argues a strange deafness to Housman's habitual rhythms.

Further evidence of such deafness on Mr. Haber's part is afforded by a fragment which he prints on page 91:

> Stand back, you men and horses,
>    You armies, turn and fly;
> You rivers, change your courses
>    And climb the hills, or I
>    Will know the reason why.
>
> Die above, O tempests brewing,
>    I will have heaven serene;
> Despair, O tides, of doing
>    The mischief that you mean,
>    For I will stand between.

The original is written, we are told, in "faded ink, beneath wavy cancellation in heavy newer ink." Did it never occur to Mr. Haber, on grounds of sound and sense, that "above" should read "down"? Is "above" so clear, beneath the heavy ink cancellation, that it

---

[1] By me in the *Observer*, February 27, 1955: "Surely, feeling (for the whole stanza breathes a sense of things coming to rest), and reason (for windows do not glisten when lights are dim), and euphony (to echo 'faded'), all cry out for 'fasten'?" I may add that Mr. John Carter read the word as "fasten," and so recorded it, when he examined the MS before it went to the United States.

was right to print it without a question-mark? Mr. Haber should
have heard the right reading even if he could not see it.

Perhaps the clearest proof of the laxity of Mr. Haber's editorial
standards is afforded by the poem printed on page 94. Mr. Haber
claims "to reproduce as closely as type allows the display and
position of the lines as they appear on the manuscript pages."
Comparison of page 94 with the facsimile of the corresponding
manuscript page shows that, as regards this page, the claim is a
false one: the printed page gives a misleading picture of the manuscript reproduced by the facsimile. How misleading, one asks, are
the pages in Mr. Haber's book for which he gives us no facsimile
to check them by? In this instance, Housman has made several
attempts at the second stanza, in different places on the page; Mr.
Haber, without giving any indication that he is doing so, gives
us a conflated version of the text, incorporating from the alternative
stanzas phrases which seem to have been rejected by the poet.

Worse than this, he reproduces falsely one of these tentative
stanzas, omitting variants and actually mistranscribing a word.
The facsimile reveals the following (we bracket and query readings
which it leaves doubtful):

> (November?)
> October comes and carries
> More than
>   Life with the leaves
>   Eternal things away
> Eternal things are (perished,?)
> The sense has left the letters
>   The tablet shall not stay
>     ir

This is how Mr. Haber presents it:

> October comes and carries
>   Life with the leaves
>   Eternal things away;
> Eternal things are perished,
> The sense has left the tablet.
>   Their tablet shall not stay.

Mr. Haber would presumably claim that his omission of two variants is justified by his own canon "Alternative readings that were canceled are generally not given." If that is accepted as an adequate defence in this particular case, we can only say that it reveals the indefensibility of the canon itself, for the variants he prints are just as much "canceled" as those that he omits. And how is Mr. Haber to justify his punctuation, and his reading "tablet" for "letters" in the penultimate line?

What would Housman himself have said of such an editor? Very much, it may be imagined, what he said of one of those who preceded him in the editing of Lucan: "[He] was a born blunderer, marked cross from the womb and perverse; and he had not the shrewdness or modesty to suspect that others saw clearer than he did." An editor can hardly be accounted shrewd if after years of study of the manuscripts he sees them less clearly, at such points as those discussed above, than a reviewer who has spent a few hours on the text with no aid beyond a couple of pages of facsimile; and even if the amendments offered here are not certainly correct, an editor who does not point out the possibility of an alternative to his own readings in contexts such as these can hardly be accounted modest. Mr. Haber certainly has not that saving grace; on only seven of the sixty pages reproduced in his Part Two does he admit the illegibility of a passage; in only five of the 500 or more lines contained in that Part does he print the "?" that marks the possible doubtfulness of his reading.

Let us turn from Mr. Haber's performance of his capital task, the presentation of the text, to observe him as a commentator on it:

> Wake; the axe of morning shatters
> Shadows through. . . .

> Wake; the roof of shadows shatters
> Splintered on the plain it spanned

The sense of these fragmentary alternatives, one would have thought, is clear enough; but Mr. Haber must needs elucidate it, with the brief note: "Here *axe* means 'axis.'" Was a sillier note, of equal length, ever penned?

Sometimes he supplements exposition with aesthetic comment:

> How much more light than morning
> That soul alive bestows
> They know not that possess it
> But he that lost it knows.

Mr. Haber devotes a footnote to telling us that "the compacted gall of this quatrain is the essence of A.E.H."

Sometimes he essays a deeper note, as when he explains the inverted commas which (in the printed text but not in the manuscript) enclose the text of "The Day of Battle": "Why," asks Mr. Haber, "were the signs of quotation added?" "Because the text is put in the mouth of an imaginary soldier," is the simple and sufficient answer. But it does not suffice Mr. Haber, who explains: "Probably as a movement of retreat from the immediacy of the grim statement of the lyric (often left out even from the 'soldiers' anthologies')." "A similar motive," he adds, "may have been behind the use of quotation marks about the heretical lyric number 47 of 'The Carpenter's Son.'" This last comment, with its naïve "heretical," shows how far Mr. Haber is from beginning to understand the temper or the idiom of his author. Since it is hardly a part of his book to expound Housman's poetry or to appraise it, this insensitiveness does not have such serious results as do those defects of which we have already given evidence. But it can lead him astray. At one point he detects a "phase of Orientalism" and at another, with equal fatuity, an "Olympian air" in Housman's poetry; and the poem that he adjudges "Olympian" he finds so reminiscent of his schoolboy verses that he is led to assign it to an early date, though it is in fact a quite ordinary example of Housman's mature rhetorical style.

Fortunately in his notes Mr. Haber confines himself for the most part to pointing out parallels and describing the actual condition of the manuscript. For such a task not much taste and not much intelligence is needed: it is enough to be able to write plain English. But plain English, unhappily, Mr. Haber is not

content to write. This is how he tells us that Housman rubbed out
or crossed out the variants that he rejected: "The inept, faltering
phrase thrown down in the haste of composition he savagely an-
nihilated with the eraser or drowned in meandering ink"; and
his description of the contents of the notebooks is enlivened by
such observations as this: "Those who put their trust in symbols
may also find it worthy of remark that the last phrase we now read
in his last notebook is 'the grave.'"

At times one wonders whether Mr. Haber's apparent inability
to write plain English may be excused by an imperfect acquaintance with the written and even the spoken language. He comments, for instance, on Housman's preference for the spelling
"shew," saying that it makes the word "a dubious rhyme with
*overflow*," and concludes that it is "probable" that Housman pronounced it "show." How else does he think that Housman could
have pronounced it? He evidently thinks that to "belabor" means
to overwork, and that "bequest" means gift; and what he thinks
he means by "obit" ("Laurence Housman's obit in the Analysis
for the majority of these fragments is 'Single lines and fragments'")
and by "omnipathy" ("an enthusiasm touched with a gleam of
omnipathy") and by "congelation" ("These few lines are further
congelations of M.P. 33") we can but guess. As for Latin—a tongue
with which an editor of Housman surely needs something more
than a nodding acquaintance—for a specimen of Mr. Haber's
competence in that language the reader may be referred to page
125.

Such solecisms as these demonstrate a lack of literacy which
might be overlooked if Mr. Haber showed a deeper understanding or appreciation of his author; but even the possession of
those attributes could not excuse the other editorial deficiencies
to which attention has been called. We are forced to conclude
that Mr. Haber exhibits what must be an almost unique combination of disqualifications for the task he has undertaken to perform.
His preface contains the hint of a possible "full-scale variorum
edition" based on the "rich material" still hidden in the Housman
notebooks. There are not a few first-rate English scholars in the
United States well qualified to prepare such an edition with the

delicacy that the task demands; if the Library of Congress intends to facilitate its appearance, and the Oxford University Press to sponsor its publication in England (as it has sponsored Mr. Haber's volume), we hope that it is to one of these that the work will be entrusted.

# Chronology of Important Dates

1859   Born on March 26 at the Valley House, Fockbury, Worcestershire.

1870–1877 Attended Bromsgrove School.

1877–1881 At St. John's College, Oxford.

1879   Gained First Class Honours in Classical Moderations, his first Public Examination at Oxford.

1881   Failed in Greats (Final School of *Literae Humaniores*), his final Public Examination, and so left Oxford without a degree. (He later qualified for a pass degree.)

1882–1892 After taking the Civil Service Examination, accepted a Higher Division Clerkship in Her Majesty's Patent Office and lived in London. During the latter years of this decade, wrote and published many papers on Greek and Latin authors.

1892–1911 Professor of Latin at University College, London.

1896   Published *A Shropshire Lad*.

1903   Published his edition of Book I of Manilius, *Astronomicon*. (Book II, 1912; Book III, 1916; Book IV, 1920; Book V, 1930.)

1905   Published his edition of Juvenal's satires.

1911–1936 Professor of Latin at Cambridge University, and Fellow of Trinity College.

1921   Lecture to the Classical Association: "The Application of Thought to Textual Criticism."

1922   Published *Last Poems*.

1926   Published his edition of Lucan.

1933   Leslie Stephen Lecture at Cambridge: *The Name and Nature of Poetry*.

1936   Died on October 30.
      *More Poems,* edited by Laurence Housman.

1937   *A.E.H.*, by Laurence Housman, which included *Additional Poems*.

# Notes on the Editor and Authors

CHRISTOPHER RICKS, the editor of this volume, is Professor of English at the University of Bristol. From 1958 to 1968 he was a Fellow of Worcester College, Oxford. He is the author of *Milton's Grand Style* (1963) and the editor of *The Poems of Tennyson* (Longmans' Annotated English Poets, 1968); he has also edited the anthology, *Poems and Critics* (1966).

KINGSLEY AMIS. Author. Among his recent books are *The Anti-Death League* (1966) and *A Look Round the Estate: Poems 1957–1967*.

W. H. AUDEN. Poet and critic.

F. W. BATESON. Fellow of Corpus Christi College, Oxford. Founder and editor of *Essays in Criticism*. Among his books are *English Poetry and the English Language* (1934), *English Poetry: a Critical Introduction* (1950), *Wordsworth: a Re-interpretation* (1954), and *A Guide to English Literature* (1965).

CLEANTH BROOKS. Gray Professor of Rhetoric, Yale University. Among his books are *Modern Poetry and the Tradition* (1939), *The Well Wrought Urn* (1947), *Literary Criticism: a Short History* (with W. K. Wimsatt, 1957), and *William Faulkner: The Yoknapatawpha Country* (1963).

CYRIL CONNOLLY. Author. Founder and editor of *Horizon*. Among his books are *The Rock Pool* (1935), *Enemies of Promise* (1938), *The Unquiet Grave* (1944), and *The Modern Movement* (1965).

RANDALL JARRELL. At the time of his death in 1966, he was Professor of English at the University of North Carolina. Among his books are *Poetry and the Age* (1953) and *Pictures from an Institution* (1954). His last book of essays was *A Sad Heart at the Supermarket* (1962), and of poems, *The Lost World* (1965).

EZRA POUND. Poet and critic.

JOHN SPARROW. Warden of All Souls College, Oxford. Among his books are *Independent Essays* (1963), *Controversial Essays* (1966), and *Mark Pattison and the Idea of a University* (1967).

J. P. SULLIVAN. Professor of Classics at the University of Texas. He is the author of *Ezra Pound and Sextus Propertius* (1964) and editor of the journal *Arion* and of the series "Critical Essays on Roman Literature."

JOHN WAIN. Author. Among his recent books are *Essays on Literature and Ideas* (1963), *The Living World of Shakespeare* (1964), *Wildtrack* (1965), and *The Smaller Sky* (1967).

RICHARD WILBUR. Professor of English at Wesleyan University. His most recent book of poems is *Advice to a Prophet* (1961); his translations include Molière's *Le Misanthrope* (1955) and *Tartuffe* (1963).

EDMUND WILSON. Man of letters.

MORTON DAUWEN ZABEL. At the time of his death in 1964, he was Professor of English at the University of Chicago. Among his books are *Literary Opinion in America* (1937) and *Craft and Character* (1957).

# Selected Bibliography

## Editions

*The Collected Poems of A. E. Housman.* London: Jonathan Cape, 1939.

Carter, John, ed., *A. E. Housman: Selected Prose.* London: Cambridge University Press, 1961. Includes Housman's "Introductory Lecture," "The Application of Thought to Textual Criticism," and "The Name and Nature of Poetry," together with a selection from his prefaces and reviews.

Haber, Tom Burns, ed., *The Manuscript Poems of A. E. Housman.* London: Oxford University Press; Minneapolis: University of Minnesota Press, 1955.

## Bibliography

Carter, John, and John Sparrow, *A. E. Housman, an Annotated Hand-List.* London: Hart-Davis, 1952.

Ehrsam, Theodore G., *A Bibliography of Alfred Edward Housman.* Boston: F. W. Faxon Co., 1941. Includes references to reviews of Housman's poetry.

Stallman, Robert W., "Annotated Bibliography of A. E. Housman: A Critical Study," *Publications of the Modern Language Association of America,* LX (1945). Evaluations of Housman's poetry and poetic theory 1920–1945.

## Biography

Gow, A. S. F., *A. E. Housman: A Sketch.* London: Cambridge University Press, 1936.

Housman, Laurence, *A.E.H.* London: Jonathan Cape, 1937.

Housman, Laurence, "A. E. Housman's 'De Amicitia,'" *Encounter*, XXIX (October, 1967).

Richards, Grant, *Housman: 1897–1936*. London: Oxford University Press, 1941.

Sparrow, John, "Housman Obscured," *Independent Essays*. London: Faber & Faber, 1963.

Watson, George L., *A. E. Housman, A Divided Life*. London: Hart-Davis, 1958.

Withers, Percy, *A Buried Life*. London: Jonathan Cape, 1940.

## Criticism

Allison, A. F., "The Poetry of Housman," *Review of English Studies*, XIX (1943).

Bishop, John Peale, "The Poetry of A. E. Housman," *Poetry*, LVI (1940). Reprinted in *Collected Essays*. New York: Charles Scribner's Sons, 1948.

Blackmur, R. P., "The Composition in Nine Poets: 1937," *The Expense of Greatness*. New York: Arrow Editions, 1940.

Bronowski, J., "A. E. Housman," *The Poet's Defence*. London: Cambridge University Press, 1939.

Brooks, Cleanth, "The Whole of Housman," *Kenyon Review*, III (1941).

Eliot, T. S., A Review of *The Name and Nature of Poetry* in *The Criterion*, XIII (1933).

Empson, William, *Seven Types of Ambiguity*. London: Chatto & Windus, 1930.

———, *Some Versions of Pastoral*. London: Chatto & Windus, 1935.

———, *The Structure of Complex Words*. London: Chatto & Windus, 1951.

———, "Rhythm and Imagery in English Poetry," *British Journal of Aesthetics*, II (1962).

Garrod, H. W., "Mr. A. E. Housman," *The Profession of Poetry*. London: Oxford University Press, 1929.

———, "Housman: 1939," *Essays and Studies*, XXV (1939).

Haber, Tom Burns, *A. E. Housman*. New York: Twayne Publishers, 1967.

Leavis, F. R., "Imagery and Movement: Notes in the Analysis of Poetry," *Scrutiny*, XIII (1945).

Marlow, Norman, *A. E. Housman, Scholar and Poet*. London: Routledge & Kegan Paul, 1958.

Orwell, George, "Inside the Whale," *Inside the Whale*. London: Victor Gollancz, 1940.

Pound, Ezra, "Mr. Housman at Little Bethel," *The Criterion*, XIII (1934). Reprinted in T. S. Eliot, ed., *Literary Essays*. London: Faber & Faber, 1954.

Ransom, John Crowe, "Honey and Gall," *Southern Review*, VI (1940).

Sparrow, John, *"A Shropshire Lad* at Fifty," *Independent Essays*. London: Faber & Faber, 1963.

Spender, Stephen, "The Essential Housman," *Horizon*, I (1940).